The HR Practitioner's Guide to Cultural Integration in Mergers & Acquisitions
Overcoming Culture Clash to Drive M&A Deal Value

The HR Practitioner's Guide to Cultural Integration in Mergers & Acquisitions
Overcoming Culture Clash to Drive M&A Deal Value

Klint C. Kendrick, Ph.D., SPHR

HR MERGERS & ACQUISITIONS ROUNDTABLE

The HR Practitioner's Guide to Cultural Integration in Mergers & Acquisitions: Overcoming Culture Clash to Drive M&A Deal Value

Copyright © 2022 by Klint C. Kendrick

All rights reserved. No part of this book may be reproduced or used in any manner without the written permission of the copyright owner except for the use of quotations in a book review.

First print editions January 2022

Illustrations by Scott Allen
DealRoom screen capture used with permission

Although the author and publisher have made every effort to ensure that the information in this book was correct at press time, neither the author nor publisher assume and hereby disclaim any liability to any party for any loss, damage, or disruption caused by errors or omissions, whether such errors or omissions result from negligence, accident, or any other cause. This book is not intended to substitute legal or professional advice, and your implementation of any suggestions set out in this book do not create a professional-client relationship. Some names and identifying details have been changed to protect the privacy of individuals and organizations.

ISBN 978-1-7349583-3-1 (hardcover)
ISBN 978-1-7349583-4-8 (paperback)
ISBN 978-1-7349583-5-5 (eBook)

Published by Mergers & Acquisitions Roundtable, LLC
www.MandARoundtable.com

MERGERS & ACQUISITIONS ROUNDTABLE, LLC

Contents

Introduction 1
Part 1: M&A Basics 15
   Chapter 1: Culture and the Deal Lifecycle 17
   Chapter 2: Strategic Basis for M&A 31
   Chapter 3: Culture Makes or Breaks Deals 45
Part 2: Causes of Culture Clash 53
   Chapter 4: Five Key Drivers of Culture Clash 55
   Chapter 5: Deal-specific Considerations 61
Part 3: Cultural Due Diligence 65
   Chapter 6: Target Screening 69
   Chapter 7: Formal Due Diligence 75
   Chapter 8: Assessing the Risk of Culture Clash 83
   Chapter 9: Communicating Cultural Due Diligence Findings 93
Part 4: Planning for Cultural Integration 99
   Chapter 10: Common Integration Scenarios 103
   Chapter 11: Aligning for Successful Culture Change 109
Part 5: Shaping the Acquired Employee Experience 117
   Chapter 12: Acquired Employee Psychology 119
   Chapter 13: Employee Communications 127
   Chapter 14: Employee Announcement Day 133

Part 6: Employee Listening 141
    Chapter 15: Pulse Surveys 145
    Chapter 16: Culture Surveys 153
    Chapter 17: Focus Groups 157
    Chapter 18: Stay Interviews 163
Part 7: The First 100 Days 169
    Chapter 19: Managing Employee Transitions 173
    Chapter 20: Onboarding Acquired Employees 181
    Chapter 21: Buddy Programs 185
Part 8: Bringing it All Together 189
    Chapter 22: A Sample Timeline 191
    Chapter 23: Measuring Cultural Integration 199
Conclusion 203
Acknowledgements 205
About the Author 207
About the HR M&A Roundtable 209
References 211

Culture eats strategy for breakfast

Attributed to Peter Drucker

Introduction

Nobody knows who actually coined the phrase "culture eats strategy for breakfast." It's frequently attributed to Peter Drucker, though the first written instance of the aphorism has been tracked to 2000, when it appeared in a newsletter overseen by Gideon Gartner (of Gartner Group fame). It resurfaced in 2006, when Mark Fields, then CEO of Ford America, said it was one of his favorite expressions. In 2008, culture's appetite got bigger, when former Merck CEO Richard Clark said, "culture eats strategy for lunch," a version of the phrase that's still popular today[1].

It doesn't matter what time of day culture decides to sit down and make a tasty meal out of strategy, the point remains that many influential business leaders understand the simple truth that no matter how good your strategy is, no matter how much you plan, no matter how lucky you get, if the culture and strategy aren't aligned, you're going to have a rough time.

Culture Clash is the Default Setting

Attending to cultural differences is especially important in the world of mergers and acquisitions. Unfortunately, this is difficult because culture is too often seen as a soft element. It's nearly impossible to capture culture on a spreadsheet, which leads some business leaders and mergers and acquisitions (M&A) professionals to dismiss it as unimportant compared to more easily quantifiable cash flows and organized project plans.

Viewing culture as a soft issue is a problem because *culture clash is the default setting.* Unless the target will be left as a standalone portfolio company, there will be changes to how work gets done, some of them quite significant. These changes generate the culture clash that causes so many deals to fail.

When leaders ignore culture, they invite culture clash to destroy deal value. Even more destructive are leaders who believe culture is just a backdoor way of coddling easily upset employees and say their newly acquired team members should "just get over it."

These value destroyers refuse to see the importance of empathy in M&A. Their egos drive them to be warrior-strategists who expand their empires through financial conquest, commanding an army of accountants and lawyers whose weapons are spreadsheets and project plans rather than blades and munitions.

These leaders often find their empires crumbling as the denizens of their newly conquered realms leave for opportunities where they feel appreciated and respected, taking tribal knowledge, paying customers, and important revenues with them. These mighty conquerors are at least partly responsible for the abysmal 80 percent failure rate we see in M&A.

To successfully overcome culture clash and preserve deal value, leaders need to act like leaders, guiding employees through the changes and challenges that naturally accompany M&A.

A Tale of Two Transactions

The criticality of overcoming culture clashes can be illustrated by two transactions I had the privilege of being part of. Both targets were acquired by the same large corporation within a few months of each other, and had similar organizational structures and business models.

To the casual observer, the key difference between these two acquisitions was the payout each company's employees received because of the deal. The first company was doing relatively well, and most employees earned at least a small payout against their outstanding stock options. The second company, on the other hand, struggled financially and employees who were expecting to make considerable money on their stock options were left empty-handed.

Introduction

You would expect that the employees who received the equity payout to be happy and likely to stay with the acquirer. Conversely, you would expect the employees who didn't receive any return on the fruits of their labor to be less satisfied with the acquisition and more likely to leave, taking important institutional knowledge, customer relationships, and years of industry experience to a competing firm.

That's exactly the opposite of what happened.

Why?

Culture!

The company that was struggling financially had a phenomenal founder who helped the integration team understand his organization's culture. The buy-side executive sponsor trusted the founder and relied heavily on him to help shape the messages we delivered to the employee base. The founder transparently explained why company leadership chose to sell the firm at such a reduced price, why he thought the sale was the best option for his team, and how involved he would be in the go-forward operations of the combined division. As a result, a significant percentage of that company's employees stayed on for the first year, allowing business leaders to focus on the business instead of re-hiring and re-training talent. The ability to focus on the business rather than on people issues was a major factor in the overall success of the deal.

In contrast, the company that was doing well had the misfortune of a buy-side business sponsor who went in with an arrogant *my way or the highway* attitude. He had done one acquisition previously and concluded that his prior approach was the only right way to do a deal. He felt it vital to give offer letters to the entire technical team, since in his mind the early offer letters were a key driver of employee retention. This was a reasonable approach, so why did it backfire?

It backfired because this business leader ignored one of the most significant cultural findings that emerged during formal due diligence. The target company had a deeply entrenched *ride or die* culture. Glassdoor reviews showed that employees who made it through the harrowing first year were likely to be lifers, spending endless hours with one another, not just at work but also during their free time. Site visits revealed employees from every department sitting at lunch together, mixing and mingling while they broke bread in a communal meal.

The camaraderie affected how products were developed and how customers were cared for. During due diligence, the R&D leader detailed how the customer support team gave critical feedback that led to product enhancements that the technical team would bring to fruition. The sales team frequently brought technical people to important client meetings. Employees were cross trained, moving smoothly between jobs and departments as part of their professional development.

Against the advice of his internal advisors, the business sponsor violated the cultural norms of the target company by creating haves and have-nots in a workplace where *we* was much more important than *I*.

His actions exacerbated the culture clash.

The acquiring leader's brash decision to extend offers to only part of the team was deeply offensive to the technical team members he so desperately wanted to keep. The hard-to-replace engineering employees left in droves. Several of them resigned without competing offers in hand, knowing their skills were in high demand and they would be employed in a matter of weeks. Customers followed these employees out the door, with more than one sales employee taking millions of dollars in future business to competitors. Value was destroyed before the deal had even closed!

In fact, at the one-year mark, the retention rate for this acquisition was the worst this large company had seen in a decade and across over 100 acquisitions, all because one leader thought his strategy could supersede the target company's culture. Ultimately, that business leader's failure to successfully complete an M&A integration that should have been relatively easy contributed to his own departure from the buy-side firm.

In this case, culture ate strategy for breakfast, the integration plan for lunch, and the business leader's career for dinner.

What is Culture?

Now that we've seen what happens when a culture is respected and when it's ignored, let's talk about what culture means in this book.

Introduction

The word *culture* came to English directly from the Latin word *colere*, meaning to till or prepare the ground for planting. Not surprisingly, this shares a root with words like cultivate and agriculture. I share this fact not only to delight my fellow word nerds, but to highlight that culture implies creating and maintaining space for something that's living, growing, and requires attention to remain strong and healthy. The best leaders go to great lengths to provide fertile ground for their organizations to live and grow so they can bear fruit.

The most used definition of organizational culture emerged in the 1980s with Dr. Edgar Schein, the Harvard- and Stanford-trained professor at the MIT Sloan School of Management. He looked at nearly a dozen definitions before landing on culture as "a pattern of shared basic assumptions[2]...". In his influential work, he goes on to describe various levels of culture that mature those basic underlying assumptions into espoused values and become cultural artifacts that include visible organizational structures and processes.

Because busy corporate executives don't typically have time or patience to read through Dr. Schein's excellent analysis of corporate culture, the definition became shortened and paraphrased, with the emphasis shifting from the organization's unseen assumptions and spoken values to those things executives could see – namely employee behaviors. This emphasis on behavior led to the pragmatic and abbreviated definition that we will use in this book. For our purposes:

Company culture is how people get things done in the workplace.

Let's explore this definition in relation to the two acquisition experiences you just read about.

In the acquisition that went well, how people got things done in that workplace was respected when a trusted founder openly shared his decision-making process. How people got things done was respected when he truthfully and humbly answered questions during the employee announcement meeting. How people got things done was respected when the target's trusted leader was given the freedom to lead his team through assimilation into the larger organization. Even though the employees were understandably disappointed that their stock options did not provide any financial rewards, they stayed because their leaders did an excellent job of transitioning how people got things done as the organization integrated.

Contrast this with the unsuccessful integration. In that workplace, the culture was *one for all and all for one!* The default culture clash worsened when the buy-side business leader created groups of haves and have-nots shortly after the deal was announced. The acquiring business leader didn't respect how people got things done in that workplace – and he paid the price.

It might be important to note that some HR practitioners (especially those with industrial/organizational psychology training like myself) go to great lengths to distinguish culture and climate. While these are indeed different constructs, the practical differences for most M&A transactions aren't sufficiently meaningful to consider in this book. Here, I use culture to refer to both organizational culture and organizational climate.

Why Can't We Get It Right?

While hubris clearly played a significant role in the demise of the deal we just discussed, even humble leaders struggle with cultural issues during M&A – and the struggle isn't new. My research on cultural integration in the M&A context has turned up references as far back as the 1960s[3]. Even with six decades of investigation into how culture affects M&A, we're no closer to consistently overcoming the culture clashes that destroy deal value.

Why is this?

First, culture is nearly all encompassing. It's difficult to know what to focus on, making it easy to ignore the issue altogether because it feels insurmountable.

This is because culture is ubiquitous. Since culture is how people get things done in an organization, it's difficult to define. It's like the air we breathe—ever-present, but hardly noticed until something unusual occurs. This makes culture difficult to measure, monitor, and change. It feels like an impossible task.

Culture is also habitual. Think about your morning commute for a moment. If you're in the United States, you know that you'll drive to

Introduction

work on the right-hand side of the road. You understand what the octagonal red sign means without needing to see the word STOP. You know how fast you can go without attracting attention and probably notice when another driver is going too fast or too slow. Your commute is a product of American driving culture.

Now imagine you're vacationing in England. You now must think twice about everything. The steering wheel is on the wrong side of the car. Even worse, you must drive on the wrong side of the road! You must keep checking the speedometer because you have no idea how fast 50 kph really is. Passing other vehicles is terrifying because you must ignore years of habit to conform to the local driving culture.

You'll eventually learn how to drive like a local, but it will take time to adjust. Acquired employees have a similar experience as they must adapt to how people are expected to get things done in their post-acquisition workplace.

Another challenge is the sheer number of thoughts, opinions, and recommendations regarding culture in M&A. An online search of "culture in M&A" returns 24,000 results. If you remove the quotes and look for pages that mention both M&A and culture, you get 48 million hits. No wonder we have a hard time figuring out where to start!

When we start to dig through these millions of pages, we find that many of them are thoughts, opinions, complaints, and criticisms, with very few actionable recommendations. We simply don't have a lot of practical solutions to the problem. I'm a voracious reader and have amassed a small library covering the people, leadership, and culture aspects of mergers and acquisitions. While I appreciate the work of my fellow authors, I find it difficult to act on most of the recommendations made in those volumes.

The Folly of Focusing on Megamergers

Another significant barrier to actionable intelligence is the focus on megamergers—those deals that get the most press due to the combination of two recognizable brands. These deals are often worth billions of dollars and involve tens of thousands of people, making it difficult to distill those lessons into typical deals, which involve only dozens of people and have valuations that are rounding errors on the balance sheets of these megalithic combined corporations.

While we can certainly learn some lessons from these titanic transactions, there are some clear limitations to applying them to the day-to-day deals most organizations experience. It's a lot like trying to learn how to do a layup by watching videos of Michael Jordan dunking the ball. Sure, its basketball, but it's probably not the best way for anybody to improve their game.

According to the Institute for Mergers, Acquisitions, and Alliances (IMAA), the average value of a deal in the United States is $189 million, and the global average deal value is $71 million[4]. This is a far cry from a megamerger, which frequently involves two firms with over $1 billion a year in revenue.

Further, according to Pitchbook, there have been over 52,000 North American M&A transactions in the last decade[5]. Contrast this with the roughly 2,000 companies in the world with sufficient revenues to even consider a megamerger[6, 7].

Government statistics tell us that of the roughly 16 million businesses in the United States, fewer than 1 percent (~170,000) employ more than 100 people, and only 0.25 percent (~42,000) have more than 500 employees[8]. This means the typical acquisition target isn't going to employ thousands of people, and most targets will have fewer than 100 employees. This dramatically smaller scale makes it likely that the average M&A deal will be far more manageable than a megamerger with tens of thousands of employees to integrate.

One of the natural shortcomings that evolves from the focus on megamergers is the emphasis on the alignment of top leaders. One article I read spent several paragraphs discussing the importance of getting the top 100 leaders together in a big ballroom so they could build relationships and get aligned. While this is critical in a megamerger, 99 percent of acquisitions don't have 100 employees, much less 100 leaders. This suggestion must be scaled to make sense for the typical deal.

The sheer size of these megamergers also makes it nearly impossible to focus on the lived experiences of individual employees and how they operate in their workplaces. They don't focus on how employees doing their day-to-day work are frequently the secret sauce of a smaller company. One or two of these key employees leaving creates a hole that value will leak through.

Contrast this with a firm employing tens of thousands of people. They might feel some pain if a few employees with critical skills leave, but the same individuals exiting a firm with 50 employees can cripple the business until replacements are found and trained. The megamerger literature can't address the real implications of employee exits due to culture clash because the threat is less existential for a larger organization.

The other reality overlooked in our obsession with megamergers is that 80 percent of all deals involve a larger firm acquiring and assimilating a smaller firm[9]. In most cases, the acquirer has a sense of what they want to do with the target company, even if they don't have specific plans. While the literature tends to evoke matrimony when discussing mergers of equals, the reality is the size and power differences create transactions that are far less collaborative than two equal-sized firms trying to sort out the best path forward.

During the many years I've been doing M&A work, I've overheard acquired leaders comparing buyers to Star Trek's Borg, a species of alien cyborgs whose catchphrase "You will be assimilated. Resistance is futile" still makes some of us shiver. If the leaders are saying these things, the rank-and-file employee is certainly not experiencing anything resembling wedded bliss!

The power imbalance between buyer and seller renders the next megamerger recommendation—a rehashing of the mission, vision, and values of the combined organization—unlikely. While a much larger firm might reshape some of their processes if the acquired company does things better, the buyer is quite unlikely to change their mission statement as the result of a deal.

Rightsizing the recommendation to host a large leadership summit for relationship and alignment building for the average deal involves acquirers showing alignment between the mission, vision, and values of the firms to re-recruit employees by highlighting where they're similar. This megamerger suggestion has now become grounded in the reality of most deals.

Finally, the megamerger approach downplays the visceral change process individual employees must go through as the two firms are combined. It ignores the reality that while culture is established at the top of the organization, it's executed by individual employees who make individual choices and take individual actions in their workplace each and every day. Managing the individual change processes of tens of thousands of people is a daunting task but leading change for the typical acquired team with fewer than one hundred people is much more achievable.

Creating a Practical Approach

To help make this book useful, I focus on the more typical, and much smaller, transactions. My goal is to provide practical, actionable advice for HR practitioners who want to do everything they can to overcome the default culture clash and drive deal value based on what's achievable in the typical transaction.

To make the book actionable, I had to select the most important concepts to include. The thousands of hours I've spent reading about, thinking about, talking about, and working on cultural integration over the last decade contain amazing insights and phenomenal suggestions but incorporating all of them into the average deal lifecycle simply can't be done. Instead, I had to rely on my own experience and the collective wisdom of other HR M&A practitioners to decide what to focus on.

Because every deal is different, this book can't contain all the answers. Instead, it aims to introduce basic proven steps you can take to overcome the default setting of culture clash. I promise you, just taking these steps will make a difference for the individuals, families, companies, and communities that are affected by M&A activity. However, some of the suggestions I chose not to include might be the perfect technique for overcoming culture clash in your transaction so don't be afraid to try new things.

Though I've spent thousands of hours working on people, leadership, and culture issues in nearly 100 deals, I don't pretend to have all the answers. So I strive to learn practical solutions from others.

This is where the HR M&A Roundtable—a community where practitioners teach practitioners how people, leadership, and culture drive M&A deal value—comes in. As the HR M&A Roundtable Chair, I have the privilege of accessing the collective wisdom of our community, which has shared cultural integration tactics based on actual experience from thousands of deals, not just the 100 I've worked on directly. To learn more about the HR M&A Roundtable and our events, you can join our mailing list by visiting www.MandARoundtable.com.

If you're reading this book, you might have attended one of our roundtables, webinars, conferences, or training programs, all focused on

Introduction

practical solutions to the problems that naturally arise in M&A. You might have read *The HR Practitioner's Guide to Mergers & Acquisitions Due Diligence*, a book that has surprisingly become required reading for new HR M&A practitioners in several organizations and was made possible because seasoned HR people are willing to share what they've learned the hard way about M&A due diligence. This book continues in that same vein, combining my firsthand experience as the HR lead on nearly 100 public and private transactions with the wisdom obtained through thousands of deals managed by members of the HR M&A Roundtable community.

While I firmly believe culture is too important to leave for HR alone, our function's focus on the manifold ways human factors affect company financial performance make us indispensable experts and advisors on company culture.

Drawing on our combined expertise allows us to embrace what celebrated leadership guru John C. Maxwell said when he wrote that "a wise person learns from his mistakes. A wiser one learns from others' mistakes. But the wisest person of all learns from others' successes.[10]"

I try to be wise enough to learn from both my own mistakes and successes as well as others' misses and hits, especially my fellow HR M&A Roundtable members. The generosity of my fellow practitioners allows this book to represent the lessons learned from billions of dollars in M&As and millions of lives touched by M&A activity. It's my sincere hope that their generosity will allow our community to make fewer mistakes and win more victories because it makes a difference in peoples' when we do M&A well.

The confidential nature of M&A work means only some details of a particular situation can be shared, even with trusted colleagues. Therefore, the stories in this book are based on actual events but have been modified or combined as needed to ensure they provide appropriate discretion while also being useful to you, the reader.

In addition, this book isn't designed to be comprehensive or exhaustive. Its primary audience isn't people who do M&A all the time. Instead, it's aimed at HR practitioners who want to do excellent work integrating two company cultures even though they have another job vying for their limited time and attention.

Finally, because I've worked primarily for U.S.-based companies, my perspective will be U.S.-centric. Even though most of the transactions

I've been part of spanned multiple regions and countries, I'm not an expert in HR or M&A in every country. You'll need to consult with appropriate local experts or attorneys before finalizing any of your cultural integration plans, especially if it means changing the terms and conditions of employment.

How This Book is Organized

This book was written with both the novice and experienced HR practitioner in mind, so the first part is a primer on the M&A process. For this reason, Part 1 includes a process overview, the strategic reasons companies engage in M&A, and some case studies that demonstrate the importance of company culture and the impact of culture clash.

Part 1 of this book is similar to Part 1 of *The HR Practitioner's Guide to Mergers & Acquisitions Due Diligence* because the basics of M&A haven't changed significantly in the two years since that book was published. To ensure this portion of the guide remains valuable to every reader, I've updated several of the case studies and shifted the emphasis from general HR matters to issues of culture. However, practitioners who read both books will note the intentional similarities in Part 1 of each book.

Part 2 shares the five key drivers of culture clash and some additional ways to evaluate how the integration might exacerbate cultural differences. In Part 3, I focus on ways the HR practitioner can identify and assess potential sources of culture clash using the information available during target screening and due diligence. The information gathered during cultural due diligence is used in integration planning, which is the focus of Part 4.

In Part 5, I shift the focus from cultural assessment and integration planning to the employee experience, which begins when employees learn about the deal on the employee announcement day. Part 6 covers four important employee listening techniques that will allow you to learn about potential cultural issues before it's too late. In Part 7, I cover several practical methods for minimizing culture clash during the integration process. Finally, in Part 8, we bring all of the ideas in this book together with a timeline and ways to measure integration success.

As you read this book, it's important to note that the M&A process is complicated and it's unlikely that the typical HR practitioner will have

Introduction

the time, capacity, or resources to take every step suggested in this guide. It's an overwhelming amount of work and very few people in full-time M&A jobs can take each of these steps on every deal. We need to carefully choose and prioritize the areas we explore and the questions we ask, trusting our instincts about the environments we work in.

My goal is for you to be able to quickly read the entire book and still feel like you've learned something practical. If you're new to M&A, I hope one day you'll show me your copy of this book, covered in your notes, highlights, and underlines. I'd like to hear both where the book helped and your thoughts on improvements when something didn't work as well as you'd hoped. If you're an experienced M&A practitioner and this book adds just one or two more practical tools to your toolbox, I'll consider that a win as well.

>Klint C. Kendrick, Ph.D., SPHR
>Chair, HR Mergers & Acquisitions Roundtable
>January 2022

Part 1: M&A Basics

As companies mature their M&A capability, people, leadership, and culture issues are increasingly viewed as essential to extracting value from M&A investments[1]. McKinsey research shows that 95 percent of corporate executives understand how critical culture is to deal success[2]. However, the transaction failure rate remains high, often due to cultural factors.

As the focus of M&A expands from pure financial modeling to include addressing the importance of culture to a successful merger, companies will need to engage people and change experts for their M&As to be successful.

The first section of this book provides context for the culture agenda, explaining the deal lifecycle, the strategic basis for M&A, and other basic M&A concepts. Once we've established a baseline understanding of how M&A works, we will discuss some culture-driven deal successes and failures, allowing you to see the difference people, leadership, and culture make in achieving deal success.

Chapter 1: Culture and the Deal Lifecycle

Before we can discuss overcoming culture clash, we need to establish a foundational understanding of how M&A works. While the M&A process can be confusing and has a lot of nuances, the big picture is quite simple. Buying a company is like buying a house.

Both buying a house and buying a company are multi-step processes that involve a number of experts. In this chapter, we provide a broad overview of each of these steps and how the processes are similar, along with basic commentary on how M&A practitioners can prepare to overcome culture clash during the deal.

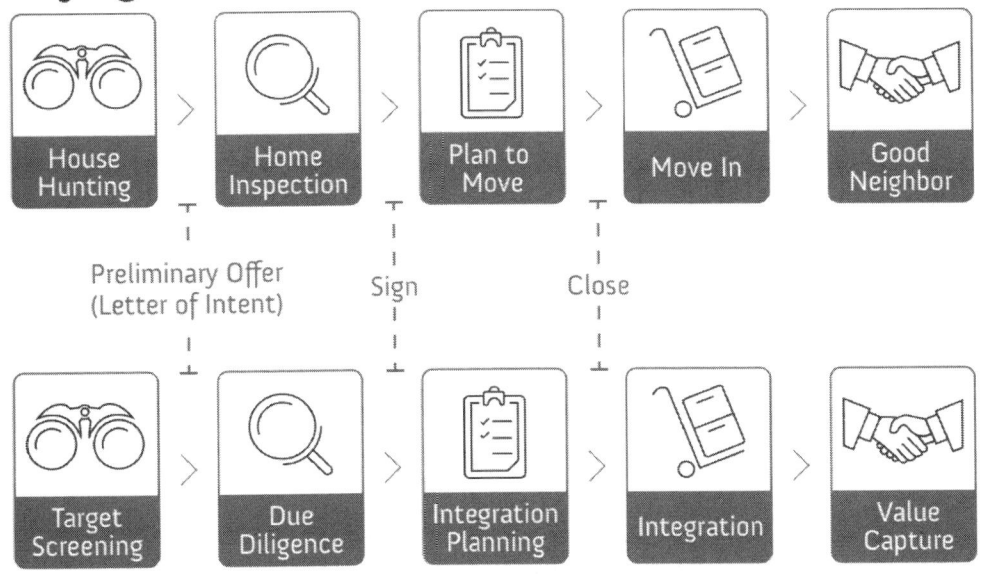

Buying A House

House Hunting > Home Inspection > Plan to Move > Move In > Good Neighbor

- Preliminary Offer (Letter of Intent)
- Sign
- Close

Target Screening > Due Diligence > Integration Planning > Integration > Value Capture

Buying A Company

17

Target Screening (House Hunting)

The first stage of the deal is frequently called target screening and occurs before the parties sign the letter of intent. This is the earliest part of the process and is similar to looking at homes and neighborhoods online, visiting open houses, and talking to a real estate agent.

At this point in the process, the buyer is usually focused on a finite number of considerations that will help them decide whether or not to make a preliminary offer. These considerations are usually limited to whether the acquisition is a good fit for the acquirer's strategy, the likely purchase price, and the target company's leadership capabilities.

Just as each homebuyer has particular needs in a house, each acquirer will have particular strategic needs for an acquisition. One homebuyer might want a starter home for their small family, another might be nearing retirement and want a more modest condominium. Yet a third buyer might be looking for a duplex so they can collect rent on half, and another buyer might be looking to get away from the city in a remote beach house or hunting cabin.

Similarly, the acquiring firm's preferred target will change depending on their goals for the M&A transaction. An acquirer might be after intellectual property, such as a brand, technology, or specific process. Qualcomm's acquisition of Nuvia, for example, was done to allow Qualcomm to incorporate 5G technology in a variety of devices in their portfolio of products[1].

A company might want to shore up their supply chain, such as when Australia's largest produce supplier Costa purchased citrus growers to ensure they could meet their customer's demand for fruit in that category[2].

The acquirer might want to purchase access to talent (what some call an acqui-hire), such as when Google purchased Bebop, reportedly to gain access to their CEO, Diane Greene, who was the former CEO of VMWare. She now leads a major Google business unit and sits on the board of Google's parent company[3].

The buyer might be seeking market access in the form of new customers, new geographies, or other opportunities to grow their revenues. Payment processing company Stripe acquired Nigerian startup Paystack to gain access to the African market[4]. Power company

Chapter 1: Culture and the Deal Lifecycle

NRG's acquisition of Direct Energy added three million retail customers and gave them access to additional markets in all 50 states and Canada[5].

It's unusual for anybody except the business sponsor and corporate development team to be involved in the target screening stage but this can be a significant error. Many acquirers screen dozens of potential targets for strategic fit, likely cost, and leadership team quality, but they tend to not pay a lot of attention to culture early on. To support future value capture, the corporate development team should add a few cultural items to the screening criteria, lest the magnitude of cultural differences be impossible to overcome, denying the opportunity to realize deal value. Chapter 6 discusses ways to incorporate cultural questions into the target screening phase.

Developing a list of culture items during target screening requires a high degree of organizational self-awareness as the acquirer must understand their own culture to create comparisons. One HR M&A Roundtable member shared how her corporate development team would always kick off formal diligence boldly asserting how highly compatible the two cultures were. She confessed to laughing aloud when the target company was a 12-person startup working from the founder's garage in western Europe. There was almost no cultural similarity between that garage startup and the gargantuan industrial with billions of dollars in annual revenues that bought them.

Letter of Intent (Preliminary Offer)

Once homebuyers find a suitable property, their agent helps them write an initial offer. In M&A, the initial offer is typically made through a letter of intent, usually referred to as an LOI. The LOI is usually non-binding, merely summarizing the proposed terms of the transaction based on the information available when the LOI is drafted. Discussing the most important items up front allows the parties to determine if crucial terms and conditions are sufficiently aligned to move the process to the formal due diligence stage.

The LOI usually focuses on proposed financial terms, including an initial proposed purchase price. It also includes the proposed deal structure, which indicates whether the buyer would prefer to purchase all of the seller's stock or just select assets. The LOI then details the next steps for the transaction, including confidentiality requirements, use of outside advisers, and the overall process and timing. In addition to the financial terms, the LOI often spells out conditions for closing the sale (such as settling pending litigation or ensuring all employees have intellectual property agreements in place), treatment of key management team members, and how the formal due diligence process will proceed.

M&A Terms – Stock and Asset Deals

- **A stock sale (also known as an equity or share sale) means the acquirer is purchasing the entire ownership stake of a whole company. In a stock sale, the new buyer assumes all of the assets and liabilities of the business.**

- **A buyer who only wants part of the company will use an asset sale. In an asset sale, assets and liabilities are more specifically delineated. They might choose this approach to avoid assuming certain liabilities, such as those related to lawsuits, severance, or product warranty claims.**

Formal Due Diligence (Home Inspection)

Once each side of the deal has decided to proceed, more people and considerations are introduced into the process. This period between LOI and deal signing is frequently referred to as formal due diligence. Think of this as a home inspection of the target company.

During formal due diligence, the target company will start to provide documents and make select employees available for interviews. Confidentiality requirements make it difficult to pull broad data from the target company during diligence, leaving the buyer to make assumptions from public data sources, meetings with disclosed employees, documents that have been provided, and site visits.

While the primary task of formal due diligence is determining if the deal should go forward and calculating a fair purchase price, due diligence items are often the only way the buyer can learn about the seller's culture and predict where culture clashes will emerge.

Convincing a company's board or owners to sell their business usually requires the buyer to pay a premium; in essence, overpaying for the business. The buyer does this because they believe they can make up the value difference through synergies. Synergies usually require making some changes to how people in the acquired business get things done.

In other words, realizing synergies requires the buyer to risk culture clashes. The earlier in the process the buyer can identify the likely sources of culture clash and plan to overcome them, the more likely they are to realize the synergies tied to deal value.

M&A Terms – Synergies

In the M&A context, a synergy occurs when the financial performance of the combined companies is better than the financial performance of each company on its own.

- **Revenue synergies happen when the combined company sells more goods and services than each company did independently.**

- **Cost synergies occur when the company spends less money to run the combined business than each company did separately. Firms often realize cost synergies through the reduction or consolidation of employees, real estate, and other business infrastructure.**

More mature acquirers understand that synergy realization requires specific planning, though research published in HBR notes that only 30 percent of deals include an effective integration plan.[6]

One of the most obvious revenue synergies, for example, is cross-selling products from each firm to one another's customers. To successfully execute on this synergy, sales teams from each side of the organization must, at a minimum, be trained on the new product offerings. However, most organizations don't include training time and costs in the integration plan, assuming the cross-sales will happen without focused effort. This also means they don't think about the culture clashes that will arise as the organization works to achieve synergies.

If the organizations choose to move forward, both the synergy plans and information gathered during formal due diligence will directly affect the integration plan, including the cultural integration. Successful navigation of the formal due diligence phase requires the buyer to overlap due diligence and integration planning, even if they must make some assumptions.

Organizations that fail to consider the need for cultural integration at this early juncture, leaving this important work until after the deal is announced, make realizing deal value orders of magnitude more difficult. Failing to attend to human issues, including culture, in a timely fashion is one of the main reasons most deals fail to meet their financial objectives. To paraphrase Benjamin Franklin, failing to plan is planning to fail.

Simply put, during the formal due diligence process, which includes early integration planning, M&A practitioners must consider how to account for people, leadership, and culture factors to make it easier for the combined business to meet its strategic objectives.

We discuss ways to incorporate cultural issues into formal due diligence in Chapter 7.

Sign and Announce

Assuming both parties agree to proceed, the next step is negotiating the final contract. This final sale and purchase agreement is often referred to as the definitive agreement and is usually a complicated set of documents that spell out nearly every portion of the transaction. These negotiations frequently require several rounds of back-and-forth between each company's attorneys before they're finally ready for signatures.

If the deal is announced to the public—and employees—when it's signed, M&A practitioners must now engage in a parallel process of initiating cultural integration while also preparing for the more robust operational integration plan. This is a remarkably busy period for most buyers, similar to a homebuyer who is simultaneously packing their old home, arranging moving companies, switching utilities, coordinating major remodeling efforts, and deciding where to put the oversized couch they hadn't fully considered when signing a daunting stack of real estate paperwork.

The employee announcement meeting is perhaps the single most important cultural event in an acquisition. That moment is the buyer's only opportunity to make a first impression. Using information gathered during formal due diligence will make this meeting go more smoothly and shows employees that the buyer respects them and is interested in their contribution to the combined company's success. We discuss the announcement meeting more in Chapter 14.

Integration Planning (Move-in Planning)

Once the deal is signed and announced to the public, the need for secrecy is greatly reduced. At this point, the buyer is able to ask more direct questions and start to coordinate more closely with the target company. There are laws governing how much collaboration is permitted before the deal closes, making it imperative to consult with deal attorneys and the corporate development team to avoid what regulators call gun-jumping.

While our homebuying process flow shows integration planning happening after the deal is signed, there is a great deal of natural overlap between formal due diligence and integration planning. In fact, some deals will have a simultaneous sign and close, in which case integration planning must occur in parallel with the formal due diligence phase.

Lifting the veil of secrecy also allows the integration team to continue cultural assessment in earnest. They now have freedom to move beyond public records, seller-provided documents, and interactions with disclosed employees. This period allows direct engagement with the seller's employee base, though this must still be handled carefully to ensure adherence to regulations and respect for acquired employee sensitivities.

Remember, firms engage in M&A so they can execute their overall business strategy. Developing a strong integration plan that considers cultural risks and opportunities will help the company achieve their strategic objectives. Cultural integration planning is the focus of Part 4.

Close

Just like a homebuyer can't remodel the house until the sale closes and they have the keys, an acquiring company can't make changes to the target company until the transaction is closed and the buyer has full management rights. M&A practitioners often refer to the final sale of the company as change in control.

Depending on closing conditions and regulatory approvals, it can take some time to close the sale and finalize change in control. Closing conditions are steps the seller must take before the buyer is willing to assume control. In a house sale, this could include bringing the plumbing or electrical system up to code. In a business sale, local law or specific contracts might require the parties to inform large customers, vital suppliers, government agencies, or employee representative bodies like works councils or unions about the sale, or even gain their consent, to close the transaction.

In some instances, the deal isn't announced to the employees until it closes. In these circumstances, the employee announcement day mentioned at the signing phase can't occur until this point in time. Furthermore, the additional cultural assessment items discussed in the section on integration planning can't commence either. This will require the M&A practitioner to simultaneously plan and execute the culture change unless integration is delayed, thereby allowing additional information gathering, a practice that has its own pros and cons.

Integration (Move-in)

Once the home sale closes, the seller hands the keys to the buyer. The buyer can then make whatever legal changes they desire. They might choose to move in immediately or they might decide to wait so they have time to decide if they really want to knock down a wall or put a pool in the back yard.

Similarly, once the deal is closed, the seller can begin executing the integration plan they started to create earlier in the M&A process. The integration plan will vary by company and deal strategy as there is seldom a one size fits all approach to integration (often called post-merger integration or PMI even if the deal isn't technically a merger). It's not uncommon for the integration plan to change during integration as the buyer gathers more information about the target company.

A well-executed integration plan requires a combination of project management and change leadership. Just like remodeling an entire home takes longer than updating the kitchen, the integration timeline will vary based on deal size and complexity. Simple integrations might only take a small group a few weeks to complete, while more complicated integrations might require large teams and several years to finalize. It's

Chapter 1: Culture and the Deal Lifecycle

not uncommon to complete some elements of an integration before others, making active change management imperative for overcoming culture clash and ensuring employees are engaged and productive during the integration period.

Remember, company culture is how people get things done in the workplace. So, if you're changing how employees interact with one another, their leaders, subordinates, external stakeholders, or even processes or tools, you've changed the culture. We discuss practical techniques for managing the cultural integration in Parts 6 and 7.

Value Capture (Good Neighbor)

Successfully completing the integration phase is the buying company's opportunity to capture the value of their investment in the new company. This is similar to the increase in a home's value when the kitchen remodel is finally done or the unfinished basement is converted to additional living space.

If the organization successfully navigated cultural integration, they are more likely to achieve the deal thesis. The organization should begin to operate with the new cultural norms in place until the next major change event occurs.

While the home buying analogy isn't perfect, it can be useful for conceptualizing the critical steps of the M&A process and is used throughout the book.

Key Roles in the M&A Process

Buying a home or company usually requires a team of experts, each of whom has a specific role to play. Different companies might use different job titles for each of the key roles in the M&A process, but it's highly likely that somebody will fill each of the functions listed in this section.

Business Sponsor

The business sponsor is the buying company executive who has directed the firm to pursue the merger or acquisition. They're responsible for understanding the business strategy and how the M&A activity will help the business achieve its strategic goals. In our example, the business sponsor is analogous to the homebuyer.

Business sponsors are often incredibly busy individuals, with broad responsibilities involving customers, suppliers, employees, and their firms. This makes it easy for some business sponsors to underprioritize the acquisition, leaving the most important deal work, including cultural integration, to other members of the deal team. This is a mistake.

Imagine for a moment a general manager letting the HR team make the final decision on their second in command or handing a contract renewal meeting with one of their five largest customers to the legal team. Leaving culture work to the deal team alone is just as irresponsible. A business sponsor who is too busy to give at least some of their time and attention to cultural integration might want to consider another business growth strategy.

This is not to say that a business sponsor must be knee-deep in the transaction at the expense of managing their already existing business. In fact, one of the smartest moves a business sponsor can make is partnering closely with the corporate development and integration management teams (each described below), relying heavily on their expertise and advise, just as a homebuyer should partner with their real estate agent and the general contractor who is their renovation project manager.

Corporate Development

The corporate development team is similar to the buyer's real estate agent. Their role is to locate and assess organizations that will help the business sponsor fulfill their strategic goals. The corporate development team typically evaluates the target for strategic fit, creates the financial model, oversees the formal due diligence process, coordinates with attorneys to negotiate contract terms, and brings the deal to close.

Chapter 1: Culture and the Deal Lifecycle

Integration Team and Leader

The integration team picks up where the corporate development team leaves off. They are responsible for supporting the business sponsor in successfully bringing the two companies together. In some companies, the corporate development and integration teams are the same group of people. In other companies there is a dedicated integration management office (or IMO).

We will refer to the person heading integration efforts as the integration leader. The integration leader is responsible for the overall acquisition project plan, managing and supporting the functional experts who will conduct the various integration workstreams. They oversee completion of overall project milestones and integration costs and might also be accountable for realizing cost and revenue synergies. Finally, they're a bridge between the business sponsor and the acquired company. Given this broad statement of work, the integration team leader should be exclusively focused on the success of the specific deal when possible and they should be brought under the tent during the target screening stage.

Research shows that effective integration leaders drive higher levels of employee retention and help businesses achieve their integration goals more quickly[7]. Effective leaders must be culturally aware and have a plethora of technical and interpersonal skills, including project management, negotiation, advocacy, and communications. The integration leader should be able to build relationships and help people on both sides of a transaction come together for their mutual success. Some organizations place high potential employees into temporary integration leader roles, using the acquisition to accelerate both business acumen and leadership competencies while simultaneously improving the odds of deal success.

Think of the integration leader as a general contractor or project manager overseeing a large renovation. Just like a general contractor directs a team electricians, plumbers, and interior designers through a remodeling project, the integration leader coordinates the functional experts in HR, IT, supply chain, and so on through the integration process. The combined group is referred to as the integration team.

The integration team is responsible for ensuring cultural alignment between the buyer and the seller. They show how work is done in the acquiring firm, partnering closely with acquired company leaders, communicating with affected employees, and modeling cultural norms and expectations. They help the acquired company integrate into the buyer's systems, translate jargon, and connect experts from the two firms.

Functional Experts

Many firms use functional experts to perform specialized due diligence and integration responsibilities. Just as a homebuyer probably doesn't want a plumber to replace the siding, the business sponsor probably doesn't want an IT expert doing sales-work. Some functional experts might be hired from the outside, like a CPA whose only job is to look at the deal financials. Others might work on both due diligence and integration, like a supplier management professional who looks at the target's vendor relationships and then helps bring the suppliers into the buyer's procurement systems.

Some larger firms separate functional due diligence teams from the functional integration teams. This model allows the company to develop deep but separate expertise in due diligence and integration, but risks losing the connection between the due diligence findings and the steps taken to mitigate those findings and ultimately realize deal value.

Functional experts are often the first to see potential culture clash because they understand how the buyer gets things done and use due diligence to learn how the seller gets things done. Their insights are critical for predicting and overcoming culture clash and they should be deliberately engaged in the cultural integration process.

Outside Experts

Most M&A transactions will include additional outside parties. Business brokers, M&A advisors, and investment bankers act like the seller's real estate agent. Each of these parties will offer different services, depending on the deal's size and regulatory requirements. Companies without an internal corporate development team might choose to use brokers, advisors, and investment bankers as buy-side agents.

Chapter 1: Culture and the Deal Lifecycle

Finally, just as more intricate real estate purchases will involve lawyers, each side of an M&A transaction will use deal attorneys who specialize in M&A. Deal attorneys might include a combination of inside and outside counsel. They might call on other attorneys, such as employment or intellectual property attorneys, to review certain aspects of the transaction and represent the best interests of their clients.

These outside experts have a more limited view of the two company cultures than individuals who work in the acquiring business but might have a unique perspective on how the two cultures will merge.

Chapter 2: Strategic Basis for M&A

Anybody who has spent more than a few hours with an M&A practitioner has probably heard the proverb "every deal is different." This accurate expression speaks to the nuances of each transaction but doesn't capture the finite number of strategic reasons organizations choose to engage in M&A activity.

For example, some firms view M&A as part of an overall growth strategy, while others use it to strengthen their product and service portfolio in small but significant ways. Others use M&A as part of an alliance strategy, allowing otherwise separate businesses to cooperate for their mutual benefit. This chapter will cover some basic concepts, but each practitioner will need to understand how their organization's leadership intends to use M&A and inorganic growth as part of their overall strategy.

The most successful practitioners understand that an acquisition is only one way of investing an organization's finite financial resources. Choosing to borrow money or spend cash on hand to fund an acquisition means the company can't allocate those same dollars on research and development, the purchase of a new manufacturing or distribution facility, increasing employee incentives, or deploying a new sales and marketing initiative. The choice to conduct an acquisition is an investment, and the goal of successful cultural integration is helping the firm realize an appropriate return on that investment.

M&A Terms – Organic and Inorganic Growth

- **Organic growth refers to how a firm's internal operations expand revenue. Organic growth strategies include increasing sales with new and different products, improved customer experiences, or increased market penetration.**

- **Inorganic growth strategies include mergers, acquisitions, joint ventures, or other alliances.**

Why Firms Buy

Firms choose to engage in inorganic growth for a variety of reasons. This section discusses many of the more common objectives of M&A. It's unusual for a company to undertake a transaction to meet just one goal. Sometimes deal objectives appear to conflict with one another and other times it seems there's no strategy at all. Furthermore, it's not uncommon for principal leaders of both the buying and selling organizations to have hidden agendas, which we discuss not with the goal of disempowering corporate leaders, but rather with an eye toward understanding how those responsible for cultural integration can influence those leaders to help ensure deal success.

M&A Term – Deal Thesis

The deal thesis describes why the acquiring organization wants to buy a specific target company. A well-written deal thesis details the business case for spending money on the potential acquisition, expected financial outcomes, and how the company plans to integrate the new business so they can realize their objectives.

Strategic and Financial Motives

Many professionals familiar with M&A categorize buyers into two groups, strategic buyers and financial buyers. While their specific objectives vary by deal (remember, every deal *is* different), their overarching acquisition strategies tend to remain the same. While we will talk about strategic and financial buyers' most typical motives for M&A, strategic buyers will sometimes do financial deals, and financial buyers will sometimes engage in strategic transactions.

Strategic buyers do deals to further their mission and vision. Strategic acquirers are usually companies that buy other companies to fold into their existing operations to some degree. Firms conduct strategic acquisitions to expand market share, gain customers, or obtain products, services, and expertise that are adjacent to their core business. Companies often cite growth as the primary reason for a strategic acquisition because inorganic growth tends to be faster than organic growth. The sudden introduction of new products and resources can make an enormous difference in a firm's gross revenues and the grim

Chapter 2: Strategic Basis for M&A

reality in most industries is that a firm must grow or die. Strategic buyers account for approximately 75 percent of U.S. deal volume each year[1].

Financial buyers, on the other hand, do deals primarily to realize a financial return. Financial buyers are often private equity or venture capital firms. They usually acquire intending to improve a business's financial metrics, like increasing cash flow or expanding operating margins. Once sufficient financial improvements have been made, they will exit that business through an initial public offering (IPO) or by divesting or selling the business to yet another acquirer. Financial buyers tend to make up the remaining 25 percent of total U.S. deal volume[2].

Both strategic and financial buyers have multiple secondary objectives for their acquisitions, and awareness of both primary and secondary objectives is critical for successful cultural integration.

If you don't feel confident that you understand why your firm is doing a deal, ask! In my experience, business sponsors and corporate development teams are typically quite happy to explain the secondary goals behind an acquisition, as all M&A success is shared success.

The remainder of this section discusses some of the key secondary objectives of M&A deals.

Cut costs

One of the biggest buzzwords in M&A is synergy. Realizing a cost synergy often means the buyer is going to reduce spending through better management practices or economies of scale. In practice, this means the firm will consolidate locations, reduce headcount, offshore jobs or production, and take other measures to make the business run more efficiently. Unless a firm is already in a cost-cutting mode, changing the cost profile of the business will necessarily create a culture change that must be managed during cultural integration.

Cost synergies were top of mind during the 2014 acquisition of Keystone Automotive Operations by alternative and specialty auto parts conglomerate LKQ. LKQ was able to slash costs by combining fleets, resulting in lower costs for delivery vehicles, gasoline, and insurance. They also eliminated overlapping warehouses and storage facilities and

33

did away with redundant positions, including both managers and delivery drivers[3].

Increase market share

A company might choose to purchase a firm with a better distribution or marketing network. This strategy makes it possible for the firm to sell their current products and services to a new group of customers. Market share increases often result in a revenue synergy, which occurs when the acquiring company can increase their income by selling products and services from both companies to one another's existing and potential customers. How employees engage with customers is a function of the corporate culture, making cultural integration an important part of a market share growth strategy.

On their third attempt, T-Mobile and Sprint merged in 2020 with a staggering $30 billion deal that took two years to clear regulatory hurdles. Nearly 55 million Sprint customers joined T-Mobile to create America's third largest wireless carrier. This rapid growth propelled the new T-Mobile to gain even more market share, leading T-Mobile to surpass AT&T Wireless and become America's second largest carrier later that same year[4].

Geographic expansion

Starting locations in a new geographic region can be a risky endeavor. Real estate, equipment, and labor costs begin to accrue in short order, but revenue takes time to materialize. There are cultural and regulatory challenges to address. It can be difficult to find leaders who can successfully work in a new location and are willing to move themselves and their families away from where they're comfortable. Purchasing a firm that's already successful in the new location can make it much faster to start offering products and services in a new location. Geographic expansion can also increase market share if the firm can introduce new customers to their products and services. Geographic expansion also carries significant culture risks as the way people get things done can vary significantly from country to country.

In 2021, Swedish fiber optic firm Hexatronic Group AB expanded into Australia with the dual purchases of The Fibre Optic Shop and Optical Solutions Australia Group[5]. These acquisitions dramatically expanded access to Australian consumers, who had previously been serviced from their New Zealand office, saving the company countless dollars and hours building infrastructure in the region. In addition to integrating distinct corporate cultures, international geographic expansion plays have the added complexities associated with bringing together differing national business cultures. Firms that place cultural integration on the back burner in global expansion deals do so at their own peril.

Accelerate innovation

Larger organizations occasionally struggle to beat smaller, more nimble competitors to market when consumers are ready for new products and services. These acquisition targets can be established companies with a new product the buyer wants, or they could be promising startups that have innovative ideas.

In an interesting and complicated deal, Ford Motor Company and Volkswagen teamed up to buy a majority share in Argo, a company that was only four months old when Ford invested $1Billion[6]. The investment came because Argo's leadership team is made up of autonomous vehicle experts from Google and Uber, and Ford needed their collective brainpower to meet their goal of having self-driving cars on the market[7].

It's likely that because innovation is at the heart of Argo's capabilities and integrating the firm into Ford's core business would change how Argo's team would work (remember our definition of culture), Argo is being left as a standalone. This approach has become increasingly common as legacy companies have historically struggled to integrate more innovative firms without generating the culture clashes that break acquired businesses and destroy deal value.

Buy strategic capabilities

Sometimes the costs of developing new technologies, products, services, areas of expertise, or resource pools are too much for a company to bear. Instead, the firm might buy a company that already has the desired capability at a price that's lower than the cost associated with building that competency in-house.

The 2019 acquisition of Talech by U.S. Bank was done to expand the big bank's digital capabilities and provide products and services that are attractive to the small and medium business market that U.S. Bank wants to attract[8].

Remove excess capacity

Economics 101 tells us that too much supply means prices go down. A company might purchase an industry competitor so they can increase prices and margins, making it possible to generate additional revenues.

Spain has more bank branches per capita than any other country in Europe, with five branches in Spain for every branch in Germany. This has led to calls for consolidation in Spain's banking sector, designed specifically to cut out excess supply and right-size the market[9]

Annihilate the competition

The best way to drive a competitor out of business might be to buy them and stop offering their products and services. The results of an annihilation strategy are like the results of a consolidation strategy.

At the time of this writing, big tech firms—including Amazon, Apple, Google, and Facebook—are facing scrutiny for M&A activity that some politicians believe was done to stifle competition. The allegation is that these firms purchased small competitors with the primary purpose of destroying companies that posed a threat to their market dominance[10]. This book isn't asserting that these companies are guilty of any wrongdoing but is simply pointing to the perceived use of this strategy as an example to enhance the reader's understanding.

M&A Terms – Horizontal and Vertical Integration

- **A horizontal merger occurs when two firms in the same industry come together to meet several elements of a deal thesis. These include increasing market share, decreasing competition, diversifying product lines, realizing economies of scale, and augmenting talent availability.**

- **Vertical integration occurs when a company buys suppliers and distribution networks related to its current business.**

Chapter 2: Strategic Basis for M&A

Real Talk: Political and Psychological Motives

There are several logical financial reasons a firm might execute an inorganic growth strategy. These reasons are usually the topics of lengthy PowerPoints and complicated spreadsheets that demonstrate how the firm will benefit financially or strategically from the purchase of a company.

Unfortunately, firms often overstate the financial reasons to engage in M&A. Analysis of 60 years of M&A transactions shows that most deals have a negative economic impact on the acquirer[11]. Perhaps this is why Harvard Business School declares between 70 and 90 percent of M&As are not merely deficient but are "abysmal failures[12]." Within the first year of a merger, 90 percent of companies lose market share[13]. Revenue growth also decreases after significant deals[14].

These financial realities mean we need to recognize that there are often other political and psychological factors at work in an acquisition. These political and psychological factors drive some business leaders to ignore the cultural risks associated with a transaction as the personal upside of doing the deal is greater than the potential downside of an integration that fails for any reason, including culture clash.

While the remainder of this book focuses on the strategic and financial motives for M&As, HR practitioners will find it meaningful to recognize the multitude of other political and psychological reasons a company leader might aggressively pursue a target.

One HR M&A Roundtable member who works in manufacturing shared an example of political motives for doing a deal. Part of his role was providing a labor cost model to the corporate development team. After including labor costs in the deal financial model, the corporate development team conceded that labor costs were going to be significantly higher than projected due to automatic pay escalators in one of the target company's collective bargaining agreements. This, in turn, would result in a much lower return on investment (ROI) than the company liked to consider when doing an acquisition.

The Roundtable member thought this realization would tank the deal, but instead, the corporate development person tweaked the synergy figures until the ROI calculation hit an acceptable number for the company's board to approve the transaction. The HR practitioner sat in stunned silence until the corporate development team member said,

37

"Look, one of our business leaders wants to do the deal, and he always gets what he wants."

This scenario is surprisingly common. A 2016 Harvard Business Review article notes that "diligence work frequently results in an overly optimistic view of the revenue synergy opportunity."[15] McKinsey research backs this up, with a survey showing that buyers only achieve 77 percent of projected revenue synergies[16].

In addition to challenges measuring the actual monetary impact of planned synergies, leaders struggle to shift the broader organization's focus and the sales team's behavior[17]. In other words, most leaders struggle to overcome culture clash. Competent people-focused leadership and updated financial incentives are often required to make changes stick, making cultural integration paramount to realizing the deal thesis.

Leaders often have psychological motives for pursuing M&A. Executives with larger organizations earn more money, which could incentivize some leaders to pursue deals[18]. Management hubris can lead to poorly diligenced and executed deals, with leaders presenting overly rosy financial justifications to the boards who approve the acquisitions[19].

As far back as 1970, researchers observed that engaging in M&A was a good PR move for executive leaders regardless of deal outcomes. Buying a company makes executives look like action-oriented leaders who take smart risks and push the organization into new frontiers[20]. The researchers noted that merely closing a transaction was often sufficient reason to attract attention from captains of industry, not only feeding the executive's ego but also lining their pockets.

These factors combine to show that simply engaging in M&A can have considerable upside for top managers. Unless the merger's results are catastrophic, a leader's reputation probably won't suffer. Research shows that well-connected CEOs who engage in bold M&As are more likely to receive CEO of the Year awards and substantial salary increases even when they destroy deal value[21].

The Oracle of Omaha, Warren Buffet, has shared his concerns that projected financial gains are seldom realistic for many M&As. In his 2014 letter to Berkshire Hathaway shareholders, he notes "A lot of mouths with expensive tastes then clamor to be fed – among them investment bankers, accountants, consultants, lawyers and such capital-reallocators as leveraged buyout operators. Money-shufflers

Chapter 2: Strategic Basis for M&A

don't come cheap."[22] His annual letters contain fantastic insight and are recommended reading for any student of M&A.

While this section might make it seem like most leaders are only motivated by self-interest when engaging in M&As, that's probably an unfair assumption. That said, it's paramount to retain a high level of political awareness and more than a bit of healthy skepticism when working on transactions, especially when it comes to gaining the support of the business sponsor to properly conduct cultural integration.

Since there's a lot to be gained by assuming our leaders and colleagues have the best intentions, the remainder of this book focuses on the strategic and financial reasons behind M&As.

Why Firms Sell

Just as there are several reasons to buy a company, there are multiple reasons to sell a business. The successful HR practitioner will be in tune with the seller's motivations. This is especially important for avoiding culture clash if the seller's key executives are continuing with the company for any length of time.

Small- and Medium-sized Businesses

The owners of small and medium businesses usually have different motives to sell their businesses than the leaders who are part of larger institutions. In many cases, executives and founders choose to part with smaller organizations because the owner or board of directors wants an exit that delivers a return on their investment of time and money.

Running a business is inherently risky, and when the company is mature enough to be sold, many owners choose to cash in on this opportunity before the market sees a downturn. They might consult with brokers and advisers to find the optimum time and ideal acquirer for their business to maximize the sale price.

Other owners find operating a business to be more demanding than is appropriate for their life circumstances. For example, they get sick or would like to retire. In cases like this, the seller often lacks a clear successor and believes selling the business is their best, or only, alternative. This approach frequently happens in family-owned businesses where the founder's children are either not ready or not willing to take over the company. In some cases, the owners would like to sell to their management team, but the management team is unable to fund the purchase.

Finally, selling to a larger organization might be an entrepreneur's goal. Many serial entrepreneurs thrive in small start-up environments and are excellent at growing businesses. These entrepreneurs have the skills to repeat their success over and over again. They sell one company and then use the funds from that sale to start another venture once the transition is complete. They might not, however, be a great cultural fit for a large organization, a dynamic that must be considered when asking for their assistance with cultural integration efforts.

Larger Organizations

The authors of *The Granularity of Growth*[23] show how a combination of acquisition and divestment activity can help organizations create portfolios that contribute to market-leading growth. As part of an overall portfolio management strategy, strategic divestment can help a business focus on its core value drivers. By shedding companies or divisions that aren't part of an organization's grand design, the seller can stop funding activity that isn't getting them where they want to go and shift those resources to the parts of the business that are most critical to their long-term strategic plan.

Tech giant IBM has used this strategy to shift their business away from making computers by selling their semiconductor business to GlobalFoundries and their server business to Lenovo[24]. This was followed by the sale of marketing platform and commerce offerings to Centerbridge Partners[25]. IBM followed with the acquisition of Red Hat[26] and the spin-off of their IT infrastructure services business[27]. All of this was done in service of transforming the 110-year-old company, which started out making punch card-reading tabulating machines for the 1890 census, to focus on higher margin hybrid cloud offerings[28].

A divestment might also occur when a seller is choosing to remove their products and services from geographic or consumer markets where their products are underperforming or are at risk due to socioeconomic or geopolitical concerns. They might find they're overextended in specific regions or product lines and believe selling part of the business is

Chapter 2: Strategic Basis for M&A

preferable to abandoning it. Shuttering a business incurs hard costs like severances and can waste assets that might be more valuable as part of a different company. For example, an empty factory might have significantly less value when sold as mere real estate than that same land and building would be worth as part of a thriving business.

In 2017, The Coca-Cola Company started selling off bottling facilities around the world, including plants in the United States, Latin America, India, and other locations where it made more sense for Coke to sell syrup to the bottler and allow a local company to manage operations[29].

Companies might also choose to sell because they need to generate cash to pay off debt or because they want to engage in a new business strategy that requires more money than they have in reserve. In these cases, divestment might be a better alternative for fundraising than finding alliance partners, taking out loans, or courting investors. In 2019, industrial conglomerate GE sold its majority share in oilfield services firm Baker Hughes specifically to pay off debt related to financial obligations[30]. This was part of a string of divestments that included GE Capital in 2015[31] and GE Healthcare in 2020[32].

A company might be legally obligated to sell off part of a business that it acquired. For example, one of the U.S. Department of Justice (DOJ) requirements for approval of the T-Mobile/Sprint merger we discussed earlier was the sale of Sprint subsidiary Boost Mobile to Dish Networks. This allowed the DOJ to feel comfortable that there would remain a fourth large cellular phone carrier in the U.S. market[33].

Finally, while it's not frequently mentioned, many companies sell off business units due to failed integration, often losing money in the process. I've personally been part of three such acquisitions, and in each case a substandard integration and subsequent mismanagement of the business resulted in sale at a lower valuation than the initial purchase price. This story is common, and in one case I met the HR person from the other side of the deal at a conference and she confessed that their firm, too, had sold off businesses that never had a chance to succeed because the cultural integration had gone so poorly.

Types of M&A Transactions

Regardless of the strategy for M&A activity, there are five basic types of transactions organizations use to meet their strategic goals. These are mergers, acquisitions, divestitures, equity investments, and joint ventures. Each of these have different implications for cultural integration.

Mergers and Acquisitions

Legally speaking, mergers and acquisitions are distinct ways of bringing legal entities together. Mergers might have tax and legal consequences (including employment law consequences) that are different from the implications of an acquisition. The legal definitions, however, are not how most people look at mergers and acquisitions, and unless the deal structure affects the culture, we won't split hairs on the technical differences.

In everyday language, *mergers* are a coming together of two equals. While the marriage of two equals reminds us of the beautiful choice two compatible people make to spend the rest of their lives together, these are business transactions. The marriage of equals rarely happens in business, as there is almost always a more dominant company either financially or culturally. The dominant company's leadership usually remains in strategic positions, though the acquirer might place a few executives from the less dominant firm into token roles. Furthermore, the culturally dominant firm often continues its management practices in the combined company, despite promises to make it the best of both worlds. In short, the honeymoon is usually over quickly, and there is trouble in paradise if the merger's cultural integration isn't handled well from the start.

Acquisitions are similar to mergers in that two companies are coming together. The term, however, might be seen as more hostile. A common perception is that the larger company is taking over the smaller organization. With an acquisition, the dominant company's management structure and business practices usually remain intact. While a takeover isn't always the case, as there are several methods for integrating an acquisition, the perception is generally accurate. Sometimes acquisitions are referred to as mergers because it evokes the

Chapter 2: Strategic Basis for M&A

marriage of equals, but the result is the same—one company has taken over another, making culture clash inevitable.

Other Related Transactions

The next three transaction types are related to mergers and acquisitions but are outside the scope of this book. Knowing the basics of these transactions can be helpful for an HR practitioner who works for a company that's interested in growing inorganically.

A *divestiture* occurs when all or part of a business is sold to another firm. It's tempting to view a divestiture as the exact opposite of a merger or acquisition. However, nothing could be further from the truth. Divestitures are complicated transactions on their own and are frequently more challenging to execute than a purchase. They can also carry significant cultural importance, especially when only part of a firm is sold off. The cultural implications of divestments are outside the scope of this book.

An *equity investment* occurs when a firm chooses to allocate funds toward another business and its activities. A company might decide to do this if a critical supplier needs help, a startup shows promise, or they would like more control over how another business operates.

Depending on the level of ownership in the equity investment, the investor might affect the culture through imposition of a governance structure required to reduce risk. While some of the cultural integration lessons of this book are applicable to majority equity investments where governance requirements are imposed on the smaller organization, thereby changing how people get things done (i.e., changing the culture), they won't be addressed specifically.

The final transaction type is a *joint venture*, frequently called a JV. In a JV, an organization invests in a strategic partnership with one or more other organizations to pursue mutually beneficial opportunities. The investment can be cash, real estate, equipment, intellectual property, people, or other assets. Companies can be majority owners, minority owners, or equal owners.

With a JV, each company usually gets representation on the JV's board of directors and some direct or indirect control of the JV's business activities. Like equity investments, cultural issues arise as two companies come together, but they aren't addressed in this book.

43

Chapter 3: Culture Makes or Breaks Deals

Global deal volume peaked in 2015, with over $5 trillion in deals completed that year[1]. In 2021, the most recent year for which we have data, total deal volume remained strong, despite the deal slowdown that occurred due to Covid. 2020 ended with $3.6 trillion in aggregate value, down only 5 percent from 2019[2] and 2021 hit $5.8 trillion[3], breaking prior records.

Despite economic and political uncertainty, KPMG expects acquisition activity to pick up in 2022 and beyond[4]. Companies are flush with cash. Record low interest rates and ready access to alternative funding sources make it easier for corporations to invest in strategic acquisitions. Private equity firms are sitting on $1.7 trillion in dry powder[5] and Goldman Sachs expects special purpose acquisition companies (SPACs) to spend more than $700 billion on M&A activity in the next two years[6]. Morgan Stanley predicts that M&A activity will pick up as pandemic-affected sectors rebound financially, believing pent-up demand will be unleashed as firms recover and retrench[7].

PwC and others predict a spate of bankruptcies as government support programs sunset[8], creating attractive distressed targets even in an era of high multiples. Cross-border deals stalled more than predicted in 2020 due to pandemic-related restrictions. This means improving public health conditions will likely unshackle suppressed demand, though overall trends indicate that more deals will remain local[9].

Growing Awareness that Culture Matters

As M&A activity has become an increasingly important part of company growth strategies, people, leadership, and culture issues are coming to the forefront as critical drivers of deal value.

Decades of research demonstrate how important it is for companies to pay attention to the human side of M&A[10] and business leaders are starting to take notice. McKinsey surveys show that 95 percent of corporate executives recognize the criticality of cultural integration to deal success[11]. Despite this awareness, a quarter of business leaders note that culture issues continue to drive deal failure[12].

Many executives continue to assert that the fundamental economic model and strong business strategy matter more than culture[13]. This either/or divide between culture and financials ignores the reality that *both* healthy culture *and* strong financials are critical to business success, even when M&A isn't part of the picture.

In addition to differences in organizational culture, significant discrepancies in how national or regional cultures operate in the background can affect deal success. A recent study showed the cultural differences between Japanese acquirers and their western target companies resulted in financial performance that was 12 percent lower than western targets acquired by western companies[14]. According to this research, Japanese firms prefer a centralized leadership approach where hard plans are made and seldom revised, whereas American and European companies tend to use less stringent roadmaps that require line managers to have more autonomy. Blending these two approaches can create additional challenges beyond those caused by organizational culture differences.

As consensus grows that cultural integration drives deal success, executives will expect HR practitioners to consider cultural impacts throughout the entire deal lifecycle, beginning at target screening and continuing through due diligence, integration planning, and into integration itself, ultimately leading to value capture.

In light of these expectations, it can be helpful to review some well-known transactions to understand how cultural dynamics make a difference. In future chapters, we will look at ways to scale lessons learned from large deals into actionable steps that will increase the likelihood that a deal will be successful. But first, let's take a brief look at some significant deals and how cultural factors led to their success or failure.

Deals That Worked

To start, here are a few classic examples of M&As that worked well due to intentional management of cultural integration.

Chapter 3: Culture Makes or Breaks Deals

Disney and Pixar

Disney's $7.4 billion acquisition of Pixar in 2006 is frequently cited as a lesson in how to manage culture in a deal. Three years before the agreement materialized, Disney and Pixar had talked about an alliance, but the clash between Disney CEO Michael Eisner and Pixar CEO Steve Jobs was too much to make the deal work. When Eisner left and Bob Iger took the Disney helm, the two firms revisited merger discussions[15].

Iger had already been through several M&A deals and understood some of the challenges that arise when cultures clash. So instead of completely assimilating Pixar, Disney treated their new acquisition as a mostly standalone operation. Decisive cultural identifiers at Pixar, like email addresses, business card titles, signage, and the casual dress code all stayed in place, keeping Pixar employees productive and engaged with minimal changes to how things got done. After some time under the House of Mouse, Disney asked Pixar leaders to step in and turn around Disney's flailing internal animation studio. Iger and Jobs had discussed this move during the early diligence phase, long before the definitive agreement was signed.

Since then, Disney acquired Marvel for $4 billion in 2009[16] and Lucasfilm for another $4 billion in 2012[17], using the same approach to managing culture. Most recently, Disney acquired 21st Century Fox's film library and other entertainment properties for $71 billion[18].

This consolidation has given Disney an indisputable hold on the box office, with five of the ten highest-grossing movies of 2020 coming from Disney's holdings[19]. Furthermore, the attractiveness of their family-friendly intellectual property helped Disney weather the pandemic that closed their parks. In only 13 months, Disney+ attracted 87 million subscribers[20], rocketing past its five-year goal of 60 million paid subscribers[21].

Enterprise and Vanguard (Alamo/National)

In 2007, Vanguard Automotive Group, then owner of the Alamo and National car rental brands, started exploring a merger with Dollar Thrifty Automotive Group, a move that would consolidate the four largest auto rental chains under one roof. Reacting quickly, Enterprise

47

Rent-A-Car made an all-cash play for their competitors and won the bid, snatching Alamo and National away from Dollar Thrifty.

Enterprise targeted people at home, including those who needed a rental while their car was in the shop. Alamo's airport locations courted discount leisure travelers and National's airport locations were favored by business travelers. Enterprise's stated goal was increasing their long-missing airport presence and taking advantage of the operational efficiencies Vanguard had worked to cultivate under private equity ownership[22].

Enterprise was already an industry disruptor, displacing Hertz as the dominant rental car company in the United States, primarily due to their customer service culture. Vanguard, on the other hand, relied on quick and efficient operations, but the customer experience was not their top priority, with the firm often ending up on the bottom of customer service lists[23].

Through deliberate management of company culture, Enterprise transformed the customer experience at Vanguard[24], while simultaneously taking Vanguard's transactional and quality assurance expertise and applying it back to Enterprise. This process was aided by thoughtful exchange of key executives between the two organizations[25].

The customer service culture was reinforced through their performance management process, with both bonuses and incentives dependent upon management team members receiving high marks from customers. Furthermore, the company created Enterprise Holdings, a unified corporate brand that allowed for consistent centralized messaging and shared resources while allowing the consumer facing brands to stand on their own[26].

Enterprise Holdings now has 44 percent of the U.S. rental car market, and continues to grow through acquisition, using the cultural lessons learned from this merger to grow their business.

Deals That Didn't Work

For every arrangement that works, there are three or four that do not. The examples below are textbook cases of failed M&As. These catastrophic failures occurred, at least in part, because leaders didn't pay sufficient attention to cultural integration. Because cultural issues were downplayed, or even ignored, executives ended up focused on people issues too late and learned the hard way that culture eats strategy for lunch.

Daimler-Benz and Chrysler

The $36 billion merger of Daimler-Benz and Chrysler was seen as a triumphant comeback for America's third-largest automobile manufacturer even though analysts thought it would be challenging from the start due to differences in culture and operating models. DaimlerChrysler would have two headquarters, one in Stuttgart, Germany and one in Detroit. German executive Juergen Schrempp would share power with Chrysler CEO Robert Eaton for some time. Executives selected London for the 1998 announcement because it was neutral ground, ensuring that neither executive upstaged the other on their home turf[27].

Unlike many megamergers, which rely on cost-cutting to compete, Daimler wanted access to production capacity outside Germany. Slow-moving Daimler was also going to learn from Chrysler's ability to get products to market much more quickly than their plodding German parent. Daimler would give its Mercedes brand broader access to American consumers through the network of Chrysler and Jeep dealerships. Industry insiders thought a well-executed deal could help Daimler compete in a global market.

Both parties rushed through the due diligence process, with the CEOs announcing the merger only weeks after the they had met again at an auto show. Some speculate the rushed deal was a reaction to a prior takeover bid by billionaire Kirk Kerkorian, whose offer made both employees and management exceptionally nervous[28]. Whatever the reason for a hurried deal, it's clear that nobody paid attention to culture issues before signing the agreement.

The takeover was swift, as top Chrysler executives fled almost immediately[29], a problem that could have been avoided by performing proper cultural diligence and mitigating leadership losses with appropriate retention packages, which would have given cultural integration a fighting chance.

Without Chrysler leaders around to hold their ground, culture clash immediately created significant challenges. Daimler's conservatism and

German national culture influenced nearly every aspect of the combined enterprise, leaving American employees unable to implement the lofty plan to expand Daimler's factory capabilities and distribution network. One dark joke asked: How do you pronounce Daimler Chrysler? The answer: It's Daimler, the Chrysler is silent[30].

In 2007, Daimler sold 80 percent of the company to a private equity firm for $6 billion, a loss of over $20 billion in value in just under ten years, primarily because culture was ignored until it was too late.

General Electric and RCA

In the 1980s, General Electric (GE) Chairman Jack Welch went on a buying spree, snapping up as many as 1,000 companies during his tenure and bringing the company from $12 billion to over $400 billion in value during his tenure[31].

One of Welch's better-known deals was the $6.4 billion acquisition of RCA, the largest non-oil acquisition in American history at the time[32]. Despite promises that the RCA acquisition would make GE an even bigger force in fields ranging from defense to consumer goods[33], it turned out that Welch really wanted NBC Television Networks, and GE sold off many of RCAs former holdings in the years following the deal.

Despite assurances that the two businesses would continue to operate separately, culture clashes immediately followed when that promise was broken. Welch assigned the former head of GE's credit division to run the network, ignoring promises made to television executives who assumed they would be in the line of succession. GE cajoled NBC managers into joining the GE political action committee as a sort of loyalty test, upsetting many key leaders. Welch expected the network to pinch pennies, even as they became one of GE's most profitable divisions, even going so far as to video tape a message threatening to fire executives who didn't toe the new company line. Most of the executives left, taking million-dollar severance packages rather than stay on with GE[34].

One of the most visible changes to the work environment occurred when a statue of Nipper, RCA's adorable canine mascot, was removed from the 30 Rock lobby. One former RCA executive provided a colorful metaphor for the acquisition, saying Welch's idea of synergy was taking a GE lightbulb and shoving it into Nipper's rear end[35].

Chapter 3: Culture Makes or Breaks Deals

The GE/RCA story ended with many legacy brands destroyed and dozens of executives fleeing, taking millions in cash severance and hundreds of millions in deal value with them, but the network did remain strong under new leadership for a decade before it slumped again. NBC has changed hands a few times, a dynamic that has been satirized in the NBC sitcom *30 Rock*, a show that includes occasional biting (and frequently accurate) commentary about the world of mergers and acquisitions.

It's easy to dismiss these billions of dollars in losses as a cost of doing business but doing so diminishes the real effect these deals had on the world. Because these deals went so poorly, thousands of people lost their jobs, billions of dollars in retirement savings were decimated, hundreds of communities had to deal with economic uncertainty, and taxpayers had to pick up the tab through bailouts and social safety programs like unemployment insurance, nutrition funding, and cash assistance.

While we can't say for certain that better cultural assessment and integration would have saved these companies, their shareholders, employees, and communities from the pain caused by these losses, firms should at least review cultural factors when deciding whether or not a deal makes sense in order to increase their chances of success.

Part 2: Causes of Culture Clash

One of the major cultural assessment and integration challenges facing HR practitioners is the extreme difficulty in operationalizing a very broad definition of workplace culture. Admittedly, the definition used in this book doesn't make this task any easier, though we repeat it here to reinforce how we're using the term.

Company culture is how people get things done in the workplace.

Because this definition is so broad, it becomes important to narrow our focus from *every* thing that happens in the workplace to the *few critical* things that will make the combined company successful.

To help overcome this challenge, in 2019 the HR M&A Roundtable charged Brendan McElroy—a graduate student researcher in his final year of The Chicago School of Professional Psychology's industrial/organizational psychology program—with developing a straightforward cultural assessment tool for our members.

To develop the assessment tool, he reviewed scores of books, articles, podcasts, and videos on the topic. He also conducted structured interviews with over a dozen HR M&A practitioners who have collectively worked on hundreds of deals affecting hundreds of thousands of employees.

These interviews turned up several key themes, all of which centered on the day-to-day interactions employees have at work. This confirmed that culture is all about how people get things done in the workplace, validating the definition used in this book.

Part 2 starts by sharing his research into the five areas of a company's culture that are most likely to exacerbate the default culture clashes that will occur in M&A. Then, because every deal is different, it provides three transaction-specific considerations HR practitioners should make part of their cultural assessment.

Chapter 4: Five Key Drivers of Culture Clash

Changing the way people get things done in the workplace is a challenge, and some changes tend to generate more culture clashes than others. As soon as an HR practitioner learns about a deal, they should begin capturing important cultural information. A method for assessing the magnitude and impact of cultural differences is introduced in Part 3. For now, our focus is on discussing the areas where culture clashes are most likely to emerge.

It's nearly impossible to create a comprehensive list of factors that might result in culture clash, but research conducted by the HR M&A Roundtable found that five key areas drive many of the culture clashes experienced during cultural integration. These areas are decision making, team collaboration, operational expectations, communication styles, and the organization's self-concept. Each of these elements exist along a spectrum, with most organizations falling somewhere in the middle rather than at one extreme or another.

While we might have personal value judgments on each of these dimensions, it's important to remember that they're neither good nor bad in the context of M&A, they're simply ways of working. The goal is to understand how an organization operates, not judge it.

Decision Making

How organizations make decisions is one of the hallmarks of their culture. Who gets to make decisions, and how the decisions are made, is one of the first areas where culture clashes arise during M&As. This is especially true when a larger process-driven company absorbs a smaller founder-driven organization.

The differences in decision rights and processes between organizations can be stark. One HR M&A Roundtable member shared the story of a founder-turned-VP who became frustrated and disillusioned shortly after selling his company to a large multinational. The founder wanted to promote one of his team members as a reward for performance. While this was a typical procedure at his company, this

HR person had to explain to him that he no longer had the authority to make personnel decisions. She explained that all promotions required approval from the CEO, and every person between the new VP and the CEO also had to approve the promotion in the company's HR system before it could take effect.

The founder was dumbstruck by the bureaucracy associated with what used to be a straightforward process and soon after experienced seller's remorse.

Six themes that will help the HR practitioner better understand the decision-making culture include:

- Who gets to make decisions, ranging from power consolidated with top executives to empowered individual contributors
- How decisions are made, with emphasis on process and consistency or an informal approach that doesn't rely on past precedent
- The level of debate permitted, ranging from swift and final decisions from top management to cultures that encourage debate or even open disagreement
- Whether decisions are made proactively, with emphasis on planning and forecasting or the needs of the moment
- The need for careful analysis backed by data, or decisions that are driven by a leader's gut feelings
- The organization's risk tolerance, where risky behaviors are either punished or celebrated

Team Collaboration

How individuals and teams collaborate is another area that can create culture clash if not managed carefully. Some organizations focus on individual efforts and successes, others focus on small groups, and still others focus on departments or the entire company.

I worked on one acquisition where the employees' favorite perk was a daily team lunch. Employees took a break every day around noon to eat together. During these lunches they would discuss both personal and professional matters. In addition to building team spirit, it was an effective way for employees to share their challenges and pull colleagues into impromptu brainstorming sessions.

Chapter 4: Five Key Drivers of Culture Clash

The business sponsor saw the value of these paid lunches and continued to fund them out of his budget, honoring the target company's culture. This decision contributed to the deal's overall success.

Six themes that highlight how organizations collaborate include:
- Whether roles and responsibilities are stable and clearly defined or employees are frequently expected to take on responsibilities that aren't associated with their position
- How the organization values deep knowledge and specialization compared to general business knowledge and the capability to have an opinion on matters worked by other functions
- Frequency and formality of structured opportunities for employees to bond
- Levels of trust between individual employees and groups
- Ways interpersonal and interdepartmental conflict is handled by leaders
- How the organization allocates limited resources to individuals and teams

Operational Expectations

The phrase *operational excellence* means different things to different organizations. For some firms, it means strict adherence to processes that have been optimized to produce high quality results for the organization and its customers. For other firms it means doing whatever it takes to get results. It's the difference between *slow and steady wins the race* and *you have to break a few eggs if you want to make an omelet*. Culture clash emerges when firms have differing ways of achieving operational excellence.

One HR M&A Roundtable member worked for a family-owned manufacturing company that had spent a decade putting Six Sigma-based process improvement into the organization, documenting how every aspect of work got done to ensure zero defects in products that were sent out the door.

When this company purchased one of their smaller suppliers, they quickly learned that the acquired CEO valued flexibility and agility. The written processes were usually suggestions and managers were encouraged to make adjustments in real time to keep the production lines moving and meet customer demand.

When the buyer integrated the acquired plant into their six sigma systems, the former owner and other employees were offended. They felt like the acquirer didn't appreciate how hard they worked to keep their customers happy. Several key leaders found other jobs, leaving the acquirer to pull people from their own manufacturing lines to make up for the resulting staffing shortages.

Six themes that help determine an organization's operational expectations include:

- How the firm deals with individuals or groups who fail to meet important goals, including whether emphasis is placed on process improvement or process compliance
- If employees are given promotions, raises, and bonuses based on tenure and adherence to company standards or are more likely to be rewarded for meeting deadlines and hitting quotas
- Whether the company prefers employees to work quickly to get things done well enough, or that they slow down slightly to ensure every process step is done perfectly
- If it's more important for employees to be on the clock and physically present for their entire shift, or if it's more important to get the work done, regardless of when and where it happens
- How often the company changes processes and structures to meet their goals
- The company's emphasis on tradition and history to explain why work gets done a certain way

Communication Styles

How and what leaders communicate is a critical element of organizational culture. This includes the frequency and tone of messages, as well as the medium.

One HR M&A Roundtable member shared how a target company's leadership communicated almost exclusively through Slack, with email being reserved for only the most formal communications. Using the cultural assessment to guide employee communications during integration, they quickly pivoted from a series of planned emails to sharing the information via a Slack channel established for the integration. They then had target company leadership review the messages and send them out directly, rather than have the messages come from the acquirer. This helped employees adjust more easily to the integration—driving higher levels of employee retention—and helped employees focus on hitting product development milestones that would have otherwise been at risk. This helped drive a successful deal.

The following six themes can help assess an organization's communication style:
- Whether leaders openly share their decision-making process or if they're more likely to convey only outcomes and provide direction
- Leadership's preference for formal messaging, like meetings or emails, as opposed to informal vehicles like Slack messages or watercooler conversations
- Frequency of broad-based employee communications
- Whether messaging is more likely to focus on the needs of customers or the needs of the organization
- The organization's tolerance for criticism and disappointing news compared to the need for all messages to be positive
- The relative importance of interpersonal skills for employees, or if rough communications are acceptable, especially by employees who are high achievers or in positions of power

Organizational Self-concept

The final area that's rife with culture clash is an organization's self-concept. This refers to how the target company sees itself and its role in the world. The organization's self-concept is often encapsulated in its mission, vision, and values statements, along with the stories and traditions it holds dear.

Rather than compare these statements and stories, we will focus on how employees behave in the workplace. Looking at how companies operationalize these values statements will explain why we want to look beyond mere words.

Consider two organizations that have both "win" and "have fun" in their values statements. The acquiring organization wins when they achieve a 30 percent margin on every sale. The target company wins when they bring on 10 new customers a month. These organizations are going to sell very differently, and the acquirer is likely to be disappointed when the target brings in new business at a 7 percent margin so they can meet their new customer targets.

Similarly, the acquiring organization has fun at the annual holiday party, when they dress up and go to a nice restaurant. The target company has fun every Friday after work when the boss pays for happy hour from 3 to 5 PM. They have quite different ideas of what fun looks like.

Six areas of organizational self-concept that can lead to culture clash include:
- How closely employees agree with and are inspired by the organization's purpose, and how that purpose might change under new ownership
- The importance of new and innovative ideas as opposed to meeting goals with proven techniques, products, and services
- Whether leaders provide mentorship, development and advancement opportunities or employees are responsible for their own career growth
- The ways in which employees feel respected and empowered in the work environment, and how that might change during integration
- Diversity, equity, and inclusion in the workplace, including visible diversity at leadership levels
- The perceived differences in social and environmental awareness between the two organizations

There are numerous opportunities for culture clash when working on a deal, but experience shows that these five areas generate a substantial number of the culture clashes that destroy deal value. By focusing on decision making, team collaboration, operational expectations, communication styles, and the organization's self-concept, the HR practitioner can zero in on the areas that are most likely to create challenges in the future.

Chapter 5: Deal-specific Considerations

The five key drivers of culture clash provide good insight into how people get work done inside a target company and are a valuable starting point for overcoming the default culture clash. However, analyzing just these five areas isn't enough to ensure cultural integration goes smoothly. To put the final changes on the HR practitioner's picture of the target company's cultural makeup, three deal-specific areas must be considered. These three areas are summed up using the three Ss: Synergies, Secret Sauce, and Sacred Cows.

To effectively assess these areas, the deal team must have at least a general sense of the desired post-deal operating model, which we discuss further in Chapter 10.

Synergies

At the tail end of the fourth merger wave, which occurred during the Reagan years, M&A researchers analyzed which deals were successful, and which were not. One of their key findings was the role of synergy capture in deal success. They found a direct correlation between the financial success of a merger and the combined firm's ability to capture synergies. In an analysis of 61 public transactions, not a single deal that failed to capture synergies hit its financial targets. Conversely, every deal that hit synergy targets also met or exceeded financial expectations[1].

The obvious overall fiscal impact of hitting or missing synergy targets creates a clear and compelling reason for synergy capture to be considered in cultural assessment. This is because in many cases realizing a synergy will require the target company to change all or part of how they do business – which means the buyer will have changed how people get things done in the workplace, risking a culture clash.

Sometimes the change won't have a significant impact on the culture, other times the change will be significant. Consider the story told in the introduction to this book. Laying off part of the target company team was necessary to realize deal synergies, but the way the layoff was conducted violated the company's culture and caused immediate value leak. Had the plan for recognizing the synergies been more thoughtfully executed, the target company probably would have enjoyed a much higher employee retention rate, resulting in better financial returns – and that business sponsor would probably not have needed to engage in his own job hunt.

A thorough culture assessment must answer the question *how will implementing the synergy plan affect the culture and the deal?*

Secret Sauce

Companies often become an acquisition target because they have some distinctive qualities that make their business special. That distinctive quality is their *secret sauce*. Sometimes the non-negotiables of the acquirer don't align with the secret sauce of the target company and become a breeding ground for culture clashes.

One HR M&A Roundtable member describes the acquisition of a small European company by an American multinational. Part of the target's secret sauce was its relationship with a local technical college, where they would recruit highly skilled entry-level workers who would remain employed for one to two years while awaiting other job opportunities. The target had astronomical rates of employee turnover, but their relationship with the technical college mitigated the turnover risk and using fresh graduates allowed them to create their products at a much lower price than their competitors. The business would change dramatically if they had to change their staffing model.

Culture clash emerged because the buyer had a much more rigorous staffing policy that was non-negotiable. Every job had to be posted on the company's website and available for anybody to apply. Every candidate had to be screened by a recruiter. Every manager had to interview at least three candidates. Every candidate had to meet with at least three interviewers. This process ballooned the time to hire, moving it from a few days to a few months. It also increased the cost of labor because entry level people were no longer the only ones considered for work.

The integration had destroyed the secret sauce of the business, causing customer deliverables to be late and dramatically changing the

Chapter 5: Deal-specific Considerations

company's cost profile and profitability. Culture clash destroyed deal value.

A thorough culture assessment must answer the question *how will changing the target's distinctive business practices (aka secret sauce) affect the deal?*

Sacred Cows

The final S to consider is the organization's sacred cows. A sacred cow typically refers to a belief that's rarely questioned and might even be immune to criticism. For purposes of cultural assessment, it's those parts of the target company's culture that are so highly valued that they should only be touched when absolutely necessary.

In many cases, the sacred cows are much loved cultural symbols. In the GE/RCA deal covered in Chapter 3, the statue of Nipper in the RCA building was a sacred cow. Removing the bronze canine from the lobby didn't change how RCA employees got their work done, but it violated the vow to leave the company as standalone, and removing Nipper became a symbol of that broken promise.

Sometimes the sacred cow is a perk or benefit. A member of the HR M&A Roundtable shared how a leader's choice to remove free refreshments at a target company created an uproar. The perk was expensive and went against the buyer's policies. However, the existing employees saw free snacks and soda as a tradeoff for their 12-hour days. When the snacks went away, productivity plummeted because the employees felt they had been cheated out of an important perk. They started to leave the office at 5:30 or 6:00 instead of staying late nights to meet deliverable deadlines. Killing the sacred cow destroyed value and dramatically increased overall costs because they needed to hire new employees who took time to ramp up and were less productive than the people who left.

A thorough culture assessment must answer the question *how will touching the sacred cows affect the deal?*

Part 3: Cultural Due Diligence

Now that we've established many of the causes of culture clash, we can turn our attention to opportunities for evaluating cultural differences in M&A.

Interest in the cultural elements of M&A seems to follow each significant M&A wave that's occurred over the past 60 years and is typically explored as organizations seek to understand why their deals failed to meet their financial targets. These attempts to understand what went wrong have led to multiple cultural assessment thought pieces, guides, tools, and checklists. Many of these tools are quite good, while others appear only fit for use in specific organizational contexts or industries.

One of the challenges associated with these tools, which are often rooted in analysis of megamergers, is an underlying assumption that deal teams or consultants can administer a single assessment after the deal has been announced, share a report of the most important cultural differences with key stakeholders, make a few adjustments to the communication plan, and then stop for the day. Nothing could be further from the truth.

The natural progression of the deal lifecycle provides many opportunities for an HR practitioner to leverage the information ecosystem and gather cultural intelligence *before* the deal is announced. The most successful acquirers take advantage of these opportunities to shape their integration plans, so they avoid culture clash and drive deal value as early as possible, including adjusting the integration plan *prior to* announcement day.

We will refer to the process of gathering cultural intelligence prior to announce as *cultural due diligence*, as gathering this information is part of the target screening and formal due diligence phases of the deal.

To refresh your recollection of the deal lifecycle, let's return to the house hunting analogy. As you recall, the first stage is target screening. The goal of this phase is to make a yes or no decision on pursuing the target company. At this point, the deal team has access to public information and a small number of seller-provided documents. The deal team's job during this phase is to identify any deal killers, including cultural deal killers, that might keep them from signing the letter of intent (LOI).

Buying A House

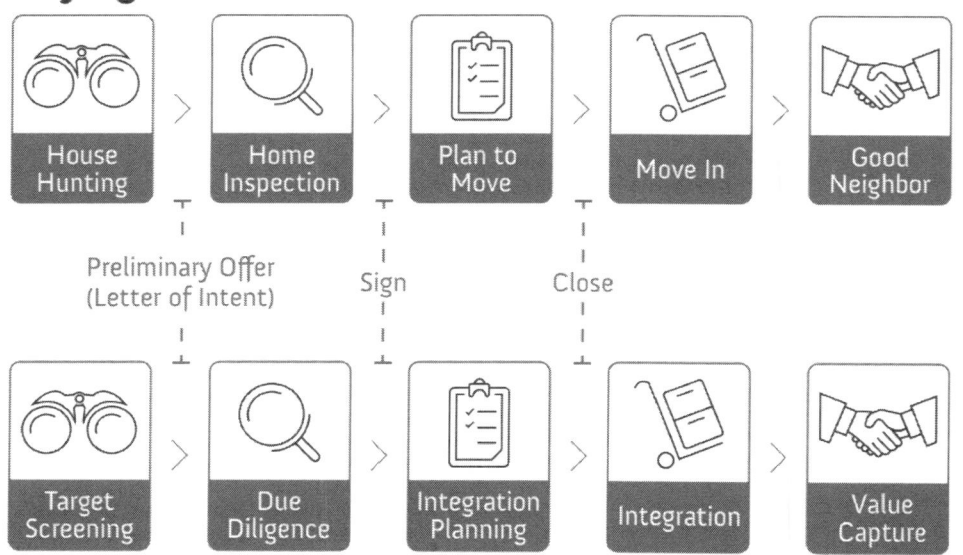

House Hunting > Home Inspection > Plan to Move > Move In > Good Neighbor

- Preliminary Offer (Letter of Intent)
- Sign
- Close

Target Screening > Due Diligence > Integration Planning > Integration > Value Capture

Buying A Company

Once the firm signs the LOI, formal due diligence begins. At this point, the deal team will gain access to additional seller-provided documents and might also conduct interviews and site visits. This is another opportunity to look for deal killers and gain valuable information that will feed forward to the integration plan. Synergy targets are often finalized during this stage, and the most successful acquirers begin to plan synergy realization in the integration plan.

Part 3: Cultural Due Diligence

Finally, the deal structure and integration model are usually informed by due diligence and finalized during the formal due diligence phase.

After the parties negotiate and sign the definitive agreement, the deal is often announced to the public and employees learn that they have a new employer. At announcement, the buyer gains significant additional access to the seller and integration planning accelerates. The buyer can now begin to gather more robust cultural information from the target company's employees, though there are limits to the kinds of contact the buyer can request with target personnel prior to the deal closing. We cover these methods in Part 6 on employee listening.

Once the deal closes and the buyer owns the target company, the buyer has access to all employees and can begin to ask for detailed information. It's at this point that most organizations deploy the robust cultural assessment tools that have been developed over the past few decades. As you can see, this is quite late in the process, and waiting to handle culture until this point in the deal can create significant challenges to preserving deal value.

Again, the most sophisticated acquirers leverage the entire deal ecosystem to gather cultural information at every stage in the deal lifecycle. Not only does this make for a smoother employee announcement day, but it allows the buyer to launch the formal cultural assessment tool in a way that respects the organization's existing culture, which they already have a basic understanding of due to the cultural intelligence they've gathered during earlier deal stages.

Finally, the HR practitioner needs to be mindful of cultural bubbles that exist in many organizations. The environment in a Los Angeles fulfillment center will probably be different than the interactions that occur in a suburban Toronto headquarters. This same dynamic can occur when leaders who sit at a North American HQ attempt to represent the culture of an entire global organization with half of its employees in Asia.

Chapter 6: Target Screening

Once a buyer decides to screen a potential target company, they should begin gathering information on the organization's culture alongside other research they conduct on the target company. This is especially true if the LOI is going to contain commitments around how the buyer will manage leadership and employee matters.

While it's unlikely that culture alone will derail a deal, cultural findings can and should inform the LOI, especially if it becomes obvious that one of the five key drivers of culture clash or a deal-specific consideration will emerge.

A member of the HR M&A Roundtable was asked to review a target company that had just gone on the market because the founder wanted to exit. During her review of public information about the target, she found multiple interviews where the target company founder shared strong negative opinions about many of the large players in their industry, including the acquirer. She immediately shared this deal-specific consideration with the corporate development team and business sponsor.

The business sponsor was still interested in the target company's products and innovation engine but knew it would be a challenge to integrate that firm into the buyer's culture. Instead, they approached the seller's bid process with a proposal that would let the target remain standalone with the founder staying on as a transitional leader for 90 days. The buyer then installed their own person as CEO and planned several years to shift the culture so smoother assimilation would be possible.

If the HR person had not conducted cultural due diligence at the target screening phase, another company would have been the successful bidder, given the founder's negative opinion of the buyer. Even if the purchase price and personal payout had been enough to overcome the founder's dislike of large companies, bringing that founder in as a VP in the larger organization would have been disastrous, resulting in yet another example of culture clash destroying deal value.

During target screening, the HR practitioner is unlikely to have access to anybody at the target company, leaving only limited opportunities to explore how the target workforce gets things done. These opportunities include public information, expert opinions, and the confidential information memorandum (CIM).

Not every firm brings HR in at target screening, which means the HR practitioner might be forced to play catch up after the LOI is signed and the formal diligence period begins. As the above example demonstrates, this is a mistake and cultural due diligence should begin before LOI to maximize deal outcomes.

Public Information

When buying a home, most people don't rely solely on the real estate agent's perspective of the neighborhood. They want to do some independent research, spending hours learning about the quality of the schools, crime rates, shopping, recreation, and other characteristics that define the area. If the buyer brings HR in at the target screening stage, they should do similar research on the target company's culture, looking for key drivers of culture clash along with their other due diligence responsibilities.

The Target Company Website

The first, and often easiest step, is reviewing the target company's website. The HR practitioner might need to coordinate these visits with the corporate development team, as multiple visits from the acquiring company's IP address could be noticed by the target company.

The About Us section is a strong place to start reviewing the website. This page usually includes information about the target's history, leadership, mission, vision, and values. The careers page also provides a rich opportunity to learn about the firm's culture, since this page includes information designed to attract future employees. Finally, some firms highlight press releases, positive media coverage, annual reports, and regulatory filings on their site.

Social and Traditional Media

Reviewing the company's official Facebook, Twitter, Instagram, Pinterest, LinkedIn, and other social media feeds can tell HR practitioners how the organization would like the public to perceive them. This content is naturally biased, making it essential to review other opinions about the target by searching for mentions or hashtags.

Glassdoor reviews can provide insight into the experience employees and job seekers have with the target company. It's not uncommon for there to be a significant disconnect between how company leadership sees itself and how the employees perceive leadership, and Glassdoor can uncover these differences. Customer review sites like Yelp or the Better Business Bureau website can provide information about how target employees interact with the public and might provide insight that HR might not uncover by looking at official feeds. It's important to note that just as a company's managed feeds tend to skew positive, review sites tend to skew negative, requiring similar levels of discernment.

Traditional media tends to be more formal than social media but can also carry similar biases. An online search of both the target company and its key leaders can be enlightening. Finally, some organizations review court records related to the target.

Expert Opinions

In addition to easily accessible public information, expert opinions can help the HR practitioner get a better sense of the target's culture.

Outside Experts

One of the most easily accessible services provided by outside experts are pre-produced reports that are available at a variety of price points. These include analyst reports, Dun & Bradstreet profiles, or other niche industry sources.

Some of the attorneys, bankers, and other advisers already involved in a transaction have industry expertise they're willing to share with buyers and can be approached to gain information on the target company's culture.

If the deal is relatively large or complicated, buyers might ask an outside firm to gather information on the target company. HR practitioners can mine reports from these competitive intelligence firms for cultural content.

In-house Experts

While many firms use outside experts during target screening and due diligence to maintain confidentiality, the buyer's own employees can be an overlooked source of competitive intelligence. If the target company is a competitor, a member of the strategy team might have previously compiled a dossier that includes cultural clues.

Some of the acquiring company's employees might have been employed by the target. The target might be a vendor, in which case the supplier management team member responsible for the relationship can provide cultural data. If the target company is a customer, the buy-side sales team could be a useful source of information about how the target company gets work done.

Because the deal is highly confidential, especially in the initial stages, in-house experts might not be as easy to approach as outside experts. To avoid potential non-disclosure issues, a general conversation about the target's industry and discussions about several competitors can help mask the potential acquisition.

The Confidential Information Memorandum

The final cultural information resource regularly available during target screening is the confidential information memorandum or CIM. This document is similar to (and sometimes called) a pitch book, teaser, or prospectus and is prepared on behalf of the target company. Though there are subtle differences between some of these documents, they can be valuable sources of cultural intelligence.

When a realtor is preparing to sell a home, they create a listing that shares basic information about the property. The listing includes the selling price, taxes and association fees, home and lot size, school and neighborhood data, and other information that will help sell the home. The listing includes beautiful photographs of the exterior and pictures

Chapter 6: Target Screening

of a well-staged interior. The narrative tells the buyer about the remodeled kitchen, local recreation, and how great it will feel once the buyer finally moves in.

In an M&A transaction, the listing is replaced by the CIM, which is often assembled on behalf of the target company by a banker or advisor who will collect a commission or fee when the business sells. The document usually opens with an executive summary that relays the value proposition of the acquisition to the potential buyer. This is followed by a brief company history and executive biographies. The next section speaks to the company's core capabilities, including information on how products and services are developed, created, sold, and provided to customers.

The next section often features a summary of industry and market opportunities, including growth potential. It highlights proprietary processes, intellectual property, critical resources, and leadership team capabilities, as the company will leverage these capabilities to exploit growth opportunities. This section might also include information on the workforce, such as headcount, critical skills, locations, and functional breakouts.

The final portion contains several years of high-level financial information, including historical data and detailed future projections. The financials occasionally include a breakdown of workforce costs.

There are situations where the target company won't create a CIM. Sometimes the target company is too small to justify the expense. The target company might only be talking to one or two firms they already know. Other times, the buyer might be initiating the process, making a CIM unnecessary. Finally, the target company might not be for sale at all, which happens in the case of a hostile takeover.

Once the HR practitioner has reviewed each of these information sources, they should analyze the data they've collected and ask what it reveals about the target company's culture and how the LOI, definitive agreement, and integration plan should be shaped to account for these findings, especially if they have identified areas of concern based on the key drivers of culture clash and deal-specific considerations.

Chapter 7: Formal Due Diligence

After the parties sign the LOI, they enter a period commonly called formal due diligence. HR is often brought into deals at this point, which means practitioners might need to complete the target screening activities outlined in the prior chapter alongside the steps detailed in this section.

During formal due diligence, HR practitioners will often gain limited access to the seller, allowing them to gather additional cultural intelligence. The information usually comes in a variety of forms, including presentations, documents, spreadsheets, interviews, and site visits. In addition to looking for key drivers of culture clash, the HR practitioner should evaluate several other risk areas during formal due diligence. You can learn more about the other risk areas in *The HR Practitioner's Guide to Mergers & Acquisitions Due Diligence*.

Seller-provided Documents

As mergers and acquisitions timelines continue to accelerate, more experienced sellers, or those sellers working with seasoned advisors, will pre-populate the virtual data room (VDR) with several types of documents. These documents usually include financial statements, regulatory filings, board resolutions, executive bios and employment agreements, compensation and benefits plans, and equity information.

As the deal proceeds, HR practitioners and other members of the deal team will usually get to request additional documents via a checklist that's shared between the parties and updated as the buyer asks for more information. The seller generally responds by placing the documents into a specific folder in the VDR and updating the checklist to show that the request has been satisfied. (You can find a checklist made by and for HR M&A practitioners on our website at www.MandARoundtable.com.)

The screen capture on the next page shows a typical folder structure inside a VDR (in this case, DealRoom). The HR folder in the VDR is often restricted to only select members of the deal team and will contain information on specific employees or plans to protect employee confidentiality.

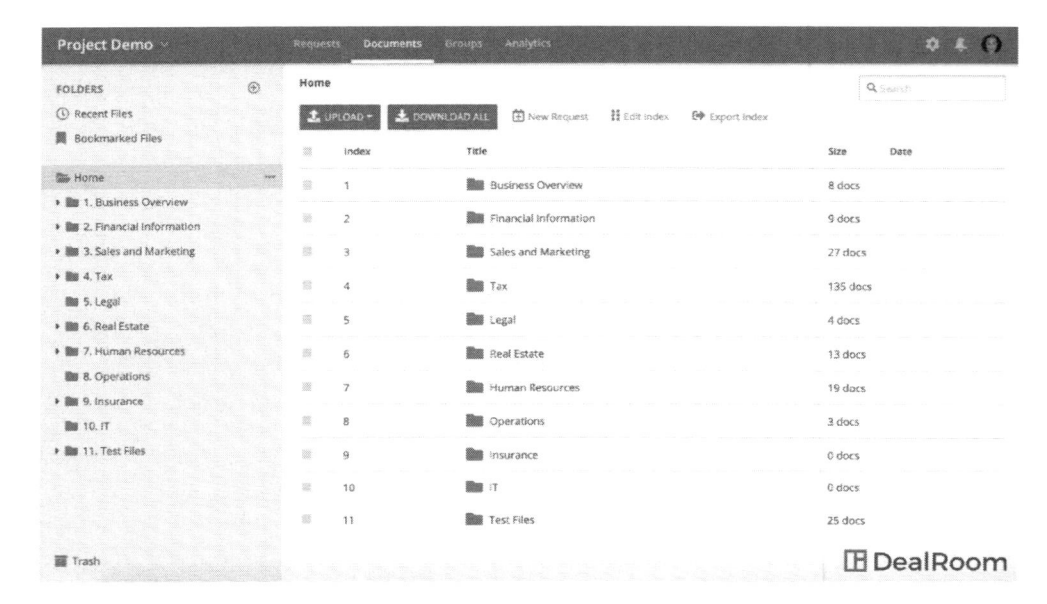

	Index	Title	Size	Date
	1	Business Overview	8 docs	
	2	Financial Information	9 docs	
	3	Sales and Marketing	27 docs	
	4	Tax	135 docs	
	5	Legal	4 docs	
	6	Real Estate	13 docs	
	7	Human Resources	19 docs	
	8	Operations	3 docs	
	9	Insurance	0 docs	
	10	IT	0 docs	
	11	Test Files	25 docs	

The VDR's contents are likely to change frequently, as information is rapidly exchanged during the fast-paced formal due diligence period. Most VDR products allow users to sign up for alerts that will inform them when the seller provides new documents. Time permitting, the savvy HR practitioner will sign up for these alerts and at least skim each item in the data room looking for culture clues.

Exploring the HR Folder

While cultural information can be found in nearly every part of the VDR, the HR folder tends to be an exceptional source of cultural intelligence. There are several documents that punch above their weight when revealing important cultural clues.

Organizational Charts

To get an immediate snapshot of the company's reporting structure and show how work is organized and prioritized, the HR practitioner should evaluate the target's organizational chart. A simple organizational chart is often included in the CIM, and more detail is frequently part of the initial VDR upload. A casual glance at the organization chart can show if the company is centralized or decentralized, flat or hierarchical, matrixed or direct. Each of these choices reflect something about the organization's culture.

Comparing which functions report directly to the CEO with which functions have leaders who are a few boxes down the chain is a decent proxy for the relative importance of the function. If the company says R&D is their most critical capability, then the head of R&D should probably report to the CEO. If that person is buried in the organization, it should generate some questions.

The same is true when looking at head count for each department. If the target says that expansion into Asia is a priority, but there are no people dedicated to that effort, it will be important to understand how they intend to meet those goals.

Headcount numbers, often included in org charts, can also be used to understand the internal political dynamics of the organization. If the CFO has a dozen direct reports, but the innovation team is limping along with only six people, it can indicate how influential those individuals are in the organization.

Finally, the org chart often contains job titles, which can reflect the relative importance of a role in the organization. If many of the CEO's direct reports are vice presidents, but the person responsible for global sales is a director, that might be a clue about how that position is perceived in the organization.

Workforce Planning

Workforce planning data includes information on turnover and open roles. Like the org chart, it shows the jobs and skills the target prioritizes and can demonstrate where the company is having challenges attracting and retaining talent.

A member of the HR M&A Roundtable learned a lot about a target company's culture when the workforce planning data revealed the firm had several mid-level supply chain roles that had been open for more than six months. She asked about these positions during the HR interview and learned that the CEO was waiting to fill these positions until they hired a new supply chain leader to replace three in a row that hadn't worked out.

Total Rewards

If you ever wonder what's important to an organization, look at how they spend their money. This is why total rewards information is a critical source of cultural intelligence. This includes both individual- and group-level rewards and the overarching total rewards structures at the target company.

At the individual level, it can be helpful to understand which senior team members are paid more, and which are paid less. This can indicate the relative importance of those individuals to the company strategy. The same is true for groups that are paid over market as compared to groups that are paid under market.

For example, if the CTO is paid significantly less than the COO, it might be reasonable to conclude that technology isn't as important to the company strategy as operations. This data should always be carefully considered, as other factors come into play when determining individual levels of pay. For example, the company might not be underprioritizing a specific role, but maybe giving somebody a developmental opportunity.

The overarching total rewards structures can also be helpful to understand. If the company has a bonus program, it's important to know what behaviors they're attempting to incentivize. For example, if the incentive is based on company or group productivity, that communicates cultural data differently than rewards that are given for individual performance.

Offer Letters and Employment Agreements

How an organization finalizes the employment offer can range from sterile facts-only paperwork to more detailed documents that are potential sources of cultural intelligence. HR practitioners should note the tone and content of the letters, as well as the consistency between letters and agreements extended to particular people or groups.

Some firms use letters that are friendly and welcoming, while others are somber and directive. Some letters include structured legal language and job descriptions, others are freeform and inconsistent. Some organizations might not even use offer letters or agreements, which also unveils something about the target company's culture.

If the target operates in multiple locations, they might have several diverse ways of extending offers and agreements to candidates, and each should be carefully reviewed.

Employee Handbooks, Policies, and Procedures

When present, handbooks, policies, and procedures can reveal a lot about an organization. Like offer letters, separate locations might have different handbooks, policies, and procedures, and each of them should be evaluated for cultural information.

These documents are designed to explain company policies, ensure legal compliance, and help employees navigate the workplace. If these documents are simply recitations of do's, don'ts, and consequences, that can be very telling about the company's culture.

On the other hand, some organizations use their handbooks to communicate important cultural information with their employees. The savvy HR practitioner should notice the tone of these documents, what they communicate about the company's values, priorities, traditions, celebrations, and how the handbooks are used to reinforce social norms in the workplace. Handbooks might also include company history, shared goals, key executive biographies, onboarding information, and other details on how things are done in the organization.

Handbooks often include total rewards information, including how people are paid, benefits, and perks. Some organizations include information on important HR processes, like talent management and diversity initiatives alongside methods for sharing ideas or suggestions with top leaders. All of these can be important resources for understanding the target's culture.

A member of the HR M&A Roundtable shared how the employee handbook revealed a clear split between office and warehouse workers within a target organization. The handbook was clearly drafted by an employment attorney and was essentially a list of prohibited practices and consequences for warehouse workers, almost all of which ended with the phrase "up to and including termination." In contrast, the handbook remained nearly silent on expectations for office-based employees.

This Roundtable member then investigated the organization's turnover rates and found that turnover in the office mirrored area averages, but warehouse turnover rates were more than double the local labor market. She hypothesized that rather than directly addressing problematic behaviors in the warehouse, the organization was hiding behind the handbook. This, in turn, led to a discussion about whether the warehouse manager was the right person for the job. This was especially important because the organization's ability to get products to customers on time was a critical value driver for the deal.

Due Diligence Interviews

Around the same time as document requests are being made, the HR practitioner should request an interview with the target company's leaders. The acquiring company is likely to hold separate meetings for each functional area, including discussions about finances, products, legal issues, and other vital matters. If the target company has an HR team, there is usually an opportunity for a practitioner-to-practitioner discussion at this point.

Due diligence interviews allow HR practitioners to ask questions that can't be answered efficiently in emails or document requests. They usually last only one or two hours and cover a variety of HR and cultural topics ranging from the target's talent philosophy, status of key leaders and employees, organizational structure, total rewards practices, performance management approach, labor and employee relations issues, and HR service delivery. Depending on the topic's sensitivity and meeting attendees, some questions might be pulled into separate discussions with a limited audience.

Due diligence interviews are often the HR practitioner's only opportunity to interact directly with the seller prior to the deal being signed, making preparation essential. This means the HR practitioner should review documents the target has already provided along with any research notes gathered during target screening (covered in Chapter 6).

Ideally, the corporate development team will provide topic areas and questions to the target in advance. Remember that this should be a genuine discussion. Intentionally aggressive or trick questions aren't helpful as the target is evaluating the buyer just as much as the acquirer is evaluating the seller. Some sellers will provide a presentation before the due diligence interview to help the conversation flow more smoothly.

Keep in mind that this is probably the first contact the target company will have with the HR practitioner, so it pays to be friendly! Formal due diligence is almost always the lowest point in the deal lifecycle since it feels like the buyer doesn't trust the seller and is asking question after question. HR practitioners can make it a little easier by being prepared and professional.

Site Visits

When circumstances allow, an in-person site visit is a unique and valuable opportunity to gain essential information about the target company's culture. Going onsite allows the HR practitioner to see the physical space and learn how the team interacts. The shift to remote work during the pandemic caused many organizations to prefer remote visits over on-site visits with future trends yet to be seen.

Careful observation can provide deep insight into the target company's culture. HR doesn't always join site visits and might need to partner with other members of the diligence team to ensure valuable information is gathered and shared.

Interviews and other interactions with business and HR leaders can help the HR practitioner learn about leader behaviors, levels of formality, communication styles, and other valuable organizational behaviors. In many cases, the site visit allows the HR practitioner to speculate about how employees will react to the acquisition.

In addition to the scheduled interviews that occur during the site visit, the team should take note of the physical space, beginning as they approach the work location. Vital information can be gleaned in the parking lot by noting signage, building condition, and who gets reserved parking spots. The welcome area reveals how the target wants customers, employees, and other visitors to perceive them.

The work environment contains many critical clues, ranging from how collaboration and privacy are managed to the artifacts the target chooses to display on their walls. Workplace perks are also a good source of cultural intelligence. Remember, how the company spends their money tells you what's important to them.

Site visits can also promote communication and lay the foundation for future cooperation, or they can alienate the leaders and employees of the acquired company. Remember, your actions during site visits and other interactions communicate important messages to the buyer. Making a positive impression will make a difference as you work through the rest of the deal lifecycle.

The Post-diligence Huddle

When a buyer is sophisticated enough to engage HR practitioners in the formal due diligence phase, they usually engage experts from multiple departments. Each function is requesting documents and meetings with the target company, asking different questions, and bringing different perspectives to the due diligence process. Sadly, most acquirers ignore the collective wisdom of the team when completing their due diligence process.

After the due diligence interviews and site visits are over, HR practitioners are strongly encouraged to harness the wisdom of the crowd, even if it means calling other due diligence leads for one-on-one discussions should the huddle be impractical for their organization.

While other topics might be discussed in this meeting, HR practitioners should ask their peers, "how will we either break or enhance the target company's business when we move employees away from their current ways of doing things and toward the end state?"

This question points right to culture, since culture is about how things get done in the workplace. Some of the target company's practices might break because of the integration. This isn't always a bad thing, as there might be room to improve how the target company does some of their work, but unintended consequences might create value leak, and that's part of what this question tries to avoid.

Chapter 8: Assessing the Risk of Culture Clash

By this stage of the transaction, the HR practitioner will have gathered significant amounts of cultural intelligence. The next step is to assess how likely it is that the default culture clash will significantly affect the deal. This, in turn, will allow the HR practitioner to update the cultural integration plan, which is the focus of Parts 4 and beyond.

A cultural risk must be relevant, likely, and material to merit attention. Most business sponsors only consider a risk relevant if it affects the deal's financial model, integration timing, company reputation, or talent retention. Likelihood refers to the probability of a risk coming to fruition. Materiality refers to the size of the risk in relation to the broader business context, including the purchase price. Culture risks can be difficult to quantify, which is one of the reasons cultural considerations are so often overlooked in M&A deals. However, using the method shared in this chapter should make it easier for the HR practitioner to demonstrate how culture risks might affect a transaction.

Culture and the Risk Assessment Matrix

The risk assessment matrix is a widely used project management tool that allows the user to visually plot the probability of a risk occurring along with the likely impact that will result if the risk comes to fruition. This tool is also frequently called a probability-impact matrix or heat map, among other names. A traditional risk assessment matrix is a five-by-five table showing the impact on one axis and the probability on the other.

If you read *The HR Practitioner's Guide to Mergers & Acquisitions Due Diligence,* you're already familiar with this tool and how it's applied to other risks that emerge during mergers and acquisitions. Like many tools, the heat map can be highly subjective, and professional judgment will have to be applied when using it.

A sample risk assessment matrix appears on the next page.

Sample Risk Assessment Matrix

	Negligible	Minor	Moderate	Major	Significant
Almost Certain	⚠️	⚠️	⊗	⊗	⊗
Likely	⚠️	⚠️	⚠️	⊗	⊗
Possible	✓	⚠️	⚠️	⚠️	⊗
Unlikely	✓	✓	⚠️	⚠️	⚠️
Improbable	✓	✓	✓	⚠️	⚠️

Impact → (horizontal axis); Probability ↑ (vertical axis)

Probability of Culture Clash

The likelihood of a disruptive culture clash arising is directly related to the degree of difference between the buyer's and target's ways of getting things done. To determine the degree of difference, the acquirer's team should start by understanding of how the future business will operate, including the integration model (discussed in Chapter 10).

To conduct this exercise, the HR practitioner should look at the five key drivers of culture clash (decision making, team collaboration, operational expectations, communication styles, and organizational self-concept), along with strategy, synergies, and sacred cows. Analyzing the information gathered during target screening and formal due diligence, the HR practitioner can rate both the buy- and sell-side cultures on a

Chapter 8: Assessing the Risk of Culture Clash

scale of zero to five. HR practitioners are encouraged to coordinate with other members of the M&A team when assigning ratings to these risks.

Once each side of the deal has a rating, calculate the difference and plot it in the risk assessment matrix. A few examples are included below, with risks beginning in 1 uncovered during target screening and risks beginning in 2 uncovered during formal due diligence. These examples will continue through this chapter.

- Risk 1.1: In the CIM, the target company shares that during the pandemic, half of their workforce moved into fully remote roles. Several workers, including two key employees, have moved away from office locations and intend to work remotely full time. The acquirer isn't comfortable with remote workers and has brought their workforce back to the office fulltime. This risk speaks to different team collaboration styles.

   The HR practitioner evaluates the cultural requirements to be physically present and assigns a value of 0 to the target and a value of 5 to the buyer. The difference is 5, which means the culture clash is almost certain to occur.

- Risk 1.2: Analysis of Glassdoor and social media mentions show target company employees are motivated by their social values, which are expressed differently than the acquiring company's social values. These are observable differences in organizational self-concept.

   The HR practitioner assigns a value of 4 to the importance of social values expression for sell-side employees and a value of 2 for buy-side employees. The difference is 2, which indicates that the culture clash is unlikely to occur.

- Risk 2.1 During the due diligence interview, the target CHRO explains that they review raises and promotions upon manager request or as a counteroffer when employees resign. The buyer, on the other hand, reviews raises and promotions on an annual cycle and doesn't generally do out of cycle raises and promotions. This is a difference in decision-making styles and operational expectations.

The HR practitioner considers the structure and formality of the seller's process and assigns a value of 2 as compared to a value of 5 for the buyer's process. The difference is 3, which makes a culture clash possible.

Impact of Culture Clash

Not all culture clashes are equal. Some culture clashes are likely to cause significant problems, while other clashes will be noisy but not painful. Once you've assessed the likelihood of culture clash emerging, you should estimate the impact. Estimating cultural impact might require the HR practitioner to imagine future scenarios. It can be helpful to engage other members of the M&A team in estimating the impacts that will occur if risks materialize.

The table below outlines one way of assigning point values to the possible impacts of culture clash, including impacts to financial outcomes, integration timing, and company reputation. The higher the point value, the more severe the consequences will be if an identified culture risk emerges.

Let's revisit our earlier examples and analyze the likely impacts if the culture clash emerges.

- Risk 1.1: In the CIM, the target company shares that during the pandemic, half of their workforce moved into fully remote roles. Several workers, including two key employees, have moved away from office locations and intend to work remotely full time. The acquirer isn't comfortable with remote workers and has brought their workforce back to the office fulltime. This speaks to differences in team collaboration styles.

    The HR practitioner rates the impact a 5. This is because employees are likely to resign if required to work from a company location. This is especially true for the two key employees who moved closer to family and will get significant deal payouts. Losing key employees is significant. Losing them could delay integration significantly, and they are both difficult and expensive to replace. In addition, other employees might exit the organization behind them.

Impact Ratings

Rating	Financial Impact	Timing Impact	Reputational Impact
5 (Significant)	More than 1% of deal value	Integration may not occur at all.	Irreparable damage to company brand. Customers and employees flee.
4 (Major)	0.5% to 1% of deal value	Integration schedule will slip significantly.	Significant damage control required. Customers and employees raise concerns in public.
3 (Moderate)	0.25% to 0.5% of deal value	The integration may be slightly delayed.	Some effort and expense required to restore customer and employee trust.
2 (Minor)	0.1% to 0.25% of deal value	Delays will be easy to recover.	Minimal damage to company brand.
1 (Negligible)	Less than 0.1% of deal value	The schedule will remain on track.	No significant impact on customer and employee perception.

- Risk 1.2: Analysis of Glassdoor and social media mentions show target company employees are motivated by their social values, which are expressed differently than the acquiring company's social values. These are observable differences in organizational self-concept.

Considering the possible outcomes of this culture clash, the HR practitioner thinks that some employees will quit, though this is unlikely to occur. The larger risk would be a significant number of employees becoming frustrated by the social values differences and choosing to make their displeasure public, which would be a major impact to the company's reputation. The impact is assigned a value of 4.

- Risk 2.1 During the due diligence interview, the target CHRO explains that they review raises and promotions upon manager request or as a counteroffer when employees resign. The buyer, on the other hand, reviews raises and promotions on an annual cycle and doesn't generally do out of cycle raises and promotions. This is a difference in decision-making styles and operational expectations.

  The HR practitioner believes this change will upset both employees and managers, as it modifies how employees are rewarded for their work. Managers will need to apply a different rigor to their recommendations and are likely to feel frustrated that promotions and raises can no longer happen on demand. This will pull manager attention from other parts of their work and could affect productivity during an adjustment period. The HR practitioner believes this adds up to a moderate impact and assigns a value of 3 to the impact of this risk.

A Sample Cultural Risk Assessment Matrix

Like all M&A due diligence, cultural due diligence occurs in phases, meaning the risk assessment matrix will be populated in phases. The sample risk assessment matrix in this chapter will help the HR practitioner to understand which risks are likely to emerge in different deal phases and how they're plotted on the matrix.

Target Screening

As discussed in Chapter 6, the objective of the target screening phase is to determine whether a preliminary offer will be made via the LOI. In

Chapter 8: Assessing the Risk of Culture Clash

addition to looking for early clues about culture clash, HR's role at this point is to identify deal killers and inputs to the financial model.

Based on HR's review of public information and the CIM, the following cultural risks are identified.

- Risk 1.1: In the CIM, the target company shares that during the pandemic, half of their workforce moved into fully remote roles. Several workers, including two key employees, have moved away from office locations and intend to work remotely full time. The acquirer isn't comfortable with remote workers and has brought their workforce back to the office fulltime.

    The risk of issues arising from this policy mismatch is almost certain (5) and the impact is significant (5) due to the likely loss of key employees and their team members.

Sample Risk Assessment Matrix

Probability \ Impact	Negligible	Minor	Moderate	Major	Significant
Almost Certain	⚠️	⚠️ 2.2	⊗	⊗ 2.3	⊗ 1.1
Likely	⚠️	⚠️	⚠️	⊗	⊗
Possible	✓	⚠️	⚠️ 2.1	⚠️	⊗
Unlikely	✓	✓ 1.3	⚠️	⚠️ 1.2	⚠️
Improbable	✓	✓	✓	⚠️	⚠️

- Risk 1.2: Analysis of Glassdoor and social media mentions show target company employees are motivated by their social values, which are expressed differently than the acquiring company's social values.

    It's unlikely (2) that the employees will choose to protest by quitting or making public statements that harm the company's reputation, but if they do the buyer would consider the impact major (4).

- Risk 1.3: When reviewing the target company's job descriptions, the HR practitioner takes note of the seller's computer stipend, where employees receive up to $3,000 to purchase the computer and peripherals that they think will best allow them to complete their work. This policy is also mentioned on LinkedIn, where several employees show off their new laptops and workstations. This is against the buyer's IT policies, which require using company-issued equipment with standard configurations, though there are sometimes exceptions allowed for special jobs.

    The HR practitioner thinks this risk is possible (3) and will have a minor impact (2) on productivity as some employees might be asked to switch to slower standard machines.

Formal Due Diligence

The formal due diligence phase gives the acquiring company additional access to the target's leaders, sites, and documents. The HR practitioner will use this information to identify potential deal killers, inputs to the financial model, or changes to the definitive agreement.

While working on formal due diligence, a few cultural risks that are relevant to the deal are discovered.

- Risk 2.1 During the due diligence interview, the target CHRO explains that they review raises and promotions upon manager request or as a counteroffer when employees resign. The buyer, on the other hand, reviews raises and promotions on an annual cycle and doesn't generally do out of cycle raises and promotions.

    The HR practitioner believes this will possibly (3) create culture clash for either employees or managers and believes this will have a moderate impact (3) on the deal as employees and managers adjust to the more rigid process.

- Risk 2.2: When reviewing the employee census file, the HR practitioner notices that most of the target's employees have job titles that include manager, director, and vice president. The acquirer restricts the use of those job titles, especially vice president, and believes most employees will be required to change them.

  The risk is almost certain to emerge (5), and the impact will be minor (2).

- Risk 2.3: During the post-diligence huddle, the buy-side procurement lead explains that target company managers usually purchase the equipment and supplies needed to create product prototypes at a local specialty store using their personal credit cards. This would be a violation of the buyer's procurement policies and will need to change shortly after the deal closes. He estimates that this change will cause the time to create prototypes to go from an average of 18 days to 45 days as they will need to complete orders in the buyer's systems, gain necessary approvals from a procurement team member, have the parts delivered to the HQ location where the supplier quality team will review the parts, and then have them shipped to the workshop area where they can then be used to build the prototype.

  The procurement process is non-negotiable to the buyer, so the risk is almost certain to emerge (5), and the impact will be major (4) as rapid prototyping is part of the target company's secret sauce.

Aligning Risks and Mitigations

As you reviewed this sample list, you might have already started thinking about ways to mitigate cultural risks. Each of these mitigations will require time and resources, which are limited and must be prioritized effectively.

To help ensure more focus is given to more significant risks, the heat map includes three zones. The first zone is represented by a check mark (√) and includes low priority items. The second zone is represented by an exclamation mark (!) and includes medium priority items. The third zone is represented by an x and includes the highest priority risks. The HR practitioner will need to exercise their best judgment and work closely with other stakeholders to determine the amount of attention each risk will receive during in the integration plan.

The remainder of the book provides several ways to mitigate cultural risks as well as proven practices for accelerating cultural integration.

Chapter 9: Communicating Cultural Due Diligence Findings

Cultural due diligence is part of the target screening and formal due diligence phases of the deal lifecycle. Therefore, it's often most efficient to communicate cultural due diligence findings at the same time as other assessments made during these early stages.

HR's responsibilities during the target screening and due diligence phases go beyond identifying potential culture clash and include five other risk areas that are covered in *The HR Practitioner's Guide to Mergers & Acquisitions Due Diligence.* These areas are often intertwined, making it inefficient for most HR practitioners to create a standalone document covering culture alone. For that reason, this book shares each of the items that are typically covered in a target screening brief or due diligence report, not just those items related to culture.

The HR practitioner should follow the conventions of the acquiring organization if there is a specific format for either the target screening brief or the due diligence report. If the firm doesn't have a format, this chapter will help HR practitioners develop templates they can use for their deals. Templates for the Target Screening Brief and Due Diligence Report are part of the Due Diligence Toolkit available from the HR M&A Roundtable's website (www.MandARoundtable.com).

Working with Limited Information

Before we discuss the report format, it's important to note that even with a thorough checklist and well-developed interview or site visit agenda, HR practitioners aren't likely to obtain enough information to feel completely comfortable with their cultural assessment.

Sellers prioritize their responses, which occasionally means answers to HR questions end up taking a back seat to strategic, operational, financial, and legal questions. The seller might not have information readily available or the team members responsible for gathering the data might not be aware of the transaction. Furthermore, the target might not feel that candid answers to HR's questions will be beneficial to their side of the transaction and might delay or filter their responses so their organization is represented in the best possible light. Whatever the reason, HR practitioners shouldn't expect to get everything they want—or need—from the seller.

When cultural information is missing, HR practitioners can extrapolate from information that's present, noting that it's an early assessment and is subject to change as more information becomes available.

M&A is inherently risky and successfully navigating the cultural due diligence process requires the ability to operate in an ambiguous environment. When data is missing, HR practitioners need to apply a high degree of professional judgment to determine the best way to communicate their findings.

Target Screening Brief

During the target screening phase, business sponsors and corporate development are deciding if they're interested enough in the target company to make an offer and what the proposed purchase price should be. The LOI often delineates how top executives will be treated, as that information can be critical for helping the seller decide if a buyer is right for them.

At this point, the HR practitioner will have extremely limited data, consisting only of public information, expert opinions, the CIM, and anything else the seller has provided. Some companies will have a preliminary integration model at this point, which HR should also keep in mind when completing the brief, including the cultural elements.

Despite HR analyzing only incomplete information, the practitioner should consider providing their analysis of each major section listed below.
- HR's opinion about proceeding with the deal.
    - Are there any HR-related deal killers? Remember, HR deal killers are rare.
    - Thoughts about deal structure. For example, are there reasons to prefer a share sale over an asset sale or vise-versa?

Chapter 9: Communicating Cultural Due Diligence Findings

- A summary of organizational information, including:
    - Approximate headcount
    - Key locations
    - Critical workforce capabilities
    - Any HR-related differentiators
- Top executives who should be specifically named in the LOI. The list is usually created in partnership with business sponsors and corporate development.
    - A brief biography of each top executive
    - Key financial and non-financial elements of the retention proposal
- If preliminary synergy plans have been developed, HR's assessment of the risks, issues, and opportunities associated with the synergy plans.
- A synopsis of key cultural characteristics that can be inferred from public information.
    - Any important cultural similarities and differences that are emerging
    - How cultural similarities and differences will affect integration and value capture

During this stage, information that's important to formal due diligence or integration planning might be discovered. The HR practitioner should retain this information so it will be available if the deal moves forward.

Formal Due Diligence Report

The formal due diligence phase is mainly used to identify potential deal killers, provide inputs to the financial model, propose changes to the definitive agreement, and shape the integration plan. The financial model includes deal synergies, which HR can help to validate during the formal diligence phase. HR will also start working on retention of key employees and the deal's integration plan, including communication and change management elements.

The HR due diligence report is a multi-page document that provides critical information on people, leadership, and culture to business sponsors, corporate development, and the integration leader. The list below includes key sections to consider including in this report.

- An update of HR's opinion about proceeding with the deal.
    - Are there any HR-related deal killers? Remember, HR deal killers are rare.
    - Thoughts about deal structure. For example, are there reasons to prefer a share sale over an asset sale or vise-versa?
- A summary of the proposed synergy plans and integration model and how it will affect people, leadership, and culture.
- A list of key employees to retain. The list is usually created in partnership with business sponsors and corporate development.
    - A brief summary of each named employee's capabilities and why they're being retained
    - Key financial and non-financial elements of the retention proposal
- Updated information about the organization, including the effects of the integration plan.
    - Current organizational structure along with any proposed changes to the organization
    - Current headcount and any changes that might occur because of the integration, including costs related to severance and recruiting if those are part of the plan
    - Key locations, including costs related to transferring employees if that's part of the plan
    - Critical workforce capabilities, including costs related to training employees if that's part of the plan
    - Any HR-related differentiators that should be included in the organizational analysis
- Other HR information that might be included in the cost model.
    - Cost impact of changes to total rewards, including the side-by-side analysis
    - Cost impact of changes to the HR service delivery model
- A summary of key HR practices, including any significant compliance risks.

Chapter 9: Communicating Cultural Due Diligence Findings

- An update to the synopsis of key cultural characteristics.
    - Any important cultural similarities and differences that are emerging
    - How cultural similarities and differences might affect integration and value capture
    - A summary of significant cultural barriers to implementing the preliminary integration model and how HR recommends overcoming these barriers
- HR's assessment of other risks, issues, and opportunities associated with the proposed synergy plans or integration models that have not already been captured.

During the formal diligence phase, HR practitioners might run across information that isn't relevant to the business sponsor or corporate development team but is relevant to the HR function. HR practitioners should keep this information handy, as it might be useful when developing and implementing the integration plan.

Part 4: Planning for Cultural Integration

Once cultural diligence is complete, the HR practitioner's attention turns to preparing for employees to learn about the deal and supporting the new team members through their change journey. While the process we've been using makes it look like integration planning happens only after the deal is signed, reality is much messier.

Buying A House

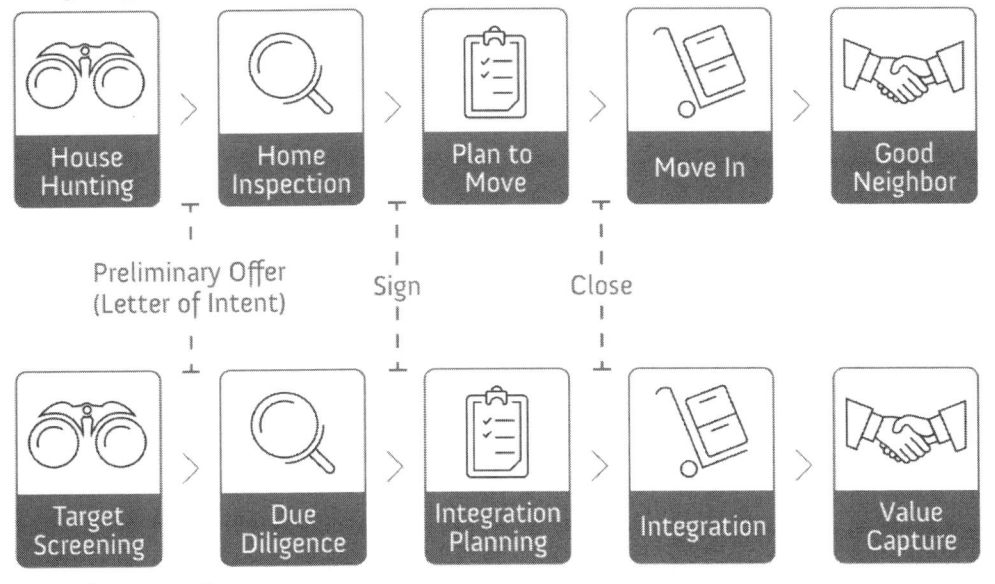

House Hunting > Home Inspection > Plan to Move > Move In > Good Neighbor

Preliminary Offer (Letter of Intent) — Sign — Close

Target Screening > Due Diligence > Integration Planning > Integration > Value Capture

Buying A Company

In most cases, integration planning starts during the due diligence process. This is like a homebuyer who starts getting estimates for the kitchen remodeling project while waiting for the home inspection report to arrive.

The duration of the integration planning period varies based on the deal. If the deal has a simultaneous sign and close, the integration planning must occur during due diligence. In other cases, there will be prolonged periods of regulatory review, like the two-year waiting period faced by T-Mobile and Sprint[1].

It's important to note that the integration plan isn't HR's responsibility. Ultimate responsibility for the integration belongs to the integration leader and business sponsor, with HR acting as an advisor on the people, leadership, and culture elements of the deal.

Cultural Integration Drives Deal Value

If an M&A transaction is like purchasing a home, integration is about what will be done with the house after the new owner gets the keys. Most people think about a home they plan to occupy differently than a home they're buying to use as a rental property. An empty nester getting a retirement home will look at their place differently than a couple expecting their third child. A property developer might not care about the house at all because they're buying a home to tear it down and subdivide the lot or build apartments on the land.

Making the most of a home purchase means knowing what's going to happen with the house. Similarly, making the most of the M&A process means knowing the final plan for the target company. While the LOI might have contemplated a company that should be tucked in or bolted on (forms of full assimilation), due diligence might find that the cultures are so misaligned that the culture clash resulting from a full integration will break the business and destroy value.

The opposite can also be true, and the buyer might decide a business isn't sufficiently led or resourced to meet deal expectations and will need to be integrated at some level. This isn't much different than a homebuyer who wanted to buy a rental property but falls in love and wants to live in their new house fulltime. The property is still a worthwhile investment, but the plan has changed, and they must consider how this change will affect the future.

One of our Roundtable members was part of an acquisition where the buyer wanted to leave the business standalone, but the selling founder wanted to retire. This led to an intense series of discussions about whether the sell-side COO was ready for the challenges of integrating and leading the business for the next several years. After much discussion, the deal team decided it would be better to integrate the business so the new leader would have more support. This example makes it clear that the integration model will have a profound impact on cultural integration.

The same is true of planning proposed synergy realization. If the deal thesis requires the elimination of overlapping locations, the integration plan should sort out how that goal will be met, including the likely magnitude of the culture clash and how to best overcome it during integration.

Failing to Plan is Planning to Fail

To thoughtfully plan for cultural integration, the buyer must have a basic idea of how the acquired company will operate after the deal is closed. While this sounds like a fairly simple proposition, and a clear end-state is supposed to be part of the deal thesis, troubling research by Harvard Business School shows that nearly 40 percent of acquirers jump into a deal with no sound reason for buying a company. Another 30 percent find three years after closing the transaction that their justifications didn't hold up. Fully 70 percent of M&A transactions lack an integration plan that will stand the test of time! [2] (If 70 percent sounds familiar, it might be because at least 70 percent of all deals fail to meet their financial objectives[3].)

In his book *Agile M&A*, Kison Patel cites several industry insiders who've seen the challenges that arise when integration plans and potential culture clash aren't considered in the initial deal thesis[4]. Throughout his book, Kison shows how seasoned acquirers see M&A as a project that starts with target screening and isn't complete until the final integration is achieved.

Leading acquirers like Google and Atlassian collaborate using the agile methods Kison recommends, but that aspirational state isn't attained by most acquiring organizations due to mismatched incentives between the dealmakers—who get paid to close deals—and integration leaders—who get paid to make the deals work out. The mismatched incentives aren't atypical. I don't know any homeowners who get regular calls from their real estate agent asking them how much they love their home!

No matter the root cause of this failure to plan for integration, the lack of a clear integration model makes it difficult for the HR practitioner to adequately plan for the employee announcement day and beyond, increasing the likelihood of culture clash emerging and festering in the absence of well-timed mitigations.

In the absence of a clear and sustainable integration plan, the HR practitioner must make some educated guesses and consider multiple scenarios. Many times, there are enough similarities between the possible integration models to proceed with a basic cultural integration plan and refine it as more information becomes available.

Chapter 10: Common Integration Scenarios

Just as there are countless possible ways to operate a profitable business, there are countless ways to successfully integrate two (or more) organizations. In this chapter, we will discuss four broad integration scenarios and their implications for culture clash.

Remain Standalone

Sometimes an acquirer will choose not to integrate a business at all. In this case, the acquired company will operate as an independent organization with its own goals, strategies, and business operations. Conglomerates, private equity firms, and other organizations that approach their holdings like a portfolio are most likely to choose this strategy. This strategy is also frequently used when the acquirer recognizes that they do not have the expertise to run the business or want to preserve the culture that has made the target company successful enough to become an acquisition target.

Going back to our real estate analogy, this dynamic is like an investor who buys an apartment building but doesn't change anything about the way it operates. The property manager continues to provide support to the tenants and uses all the existing vendors to keep the property in good repair. The only thing the property manager changes is where tenants send the rents.

Microsoft's 2016 acquisition of LinkedIn is an example of leaving a business to stand alone. While many pundits were skeptical that Microsoft would leave LinkedIn independent, they have kept that promise, leaving LinkedIn to thrive, holding onto the leaders and culture that made it successful. The synergies come through integrations between various Microsoft and LinkedIn products, such as moving LinkedIn to Microsoft's Azure Cloud servers and the ability for users to connect their LinkedIn networks to their Microsoft Outlook accounts[1].

Standalone organizations are at the least risk of culture clash, but they're not immune to it. Different governance requirements and strategic expectations will change how the target company does business, which means there will be some change in company culture.

One Roundtable member discussed how frustrated an acquired founder felt when the acquirer insisted the founder's brother could no longer be the target's CFO. The acquirer's financial control policies didn't allow relatives to oversee one another's spending. The acquirer found another finance position for the founder's brother, but resentment over the forced change lingered for years.

Partially Integrate

Partial integration occurs when the acquirer chooses to pull some functions into the parent organization while leaving other aspects to be managed by the sell-side company. For example, back-office functions like HR, IT, and finance might be taken over by the parent company while the sell-side leadership team maintains control of R&D, manufacturing, distribution, marketing, and sales.

In our real estate analogy, an investor buys an apartment building and keeps the building manager in place to help tenants and collect rents but changes the maintenance and landscaping service.

TCS Education System is a private non-profit college system that uses this strategy. Their holdings include The Chicago School of Professional Psychology (of which I'm an alum), Pacific Oaks College, Saybrook University, Kansas Health Science Center, and the Santa Barbara and Ventura Colleges of Law. TCS provides several shared services to their affiliated universities and the students, including admissions, accreditation support, and shared finance, IT and HR services[2]. Each college in the system has its own president and board and maintains control over its faculty and academic offerings[3].

Culture clashes are likely to emerge in partial integration scenarios. In addition to the changes in strategy and leadership that will occur due to the acquisition, culture clashes abound when teams are split up and systems and processes are changed.

A Roundtable member worked for a company that partially integrated most of their acquisitions, insisting on a shared back office to save costs and ensure compliance with company policy. This move did save money, but target company leaders frequently complained that they needed to add two additional employees to project manage the additional bureaucracy the partial integration created.

Fully Assimilate

Full integration occurs when the buyer absorbs the entire acquired organization into its policies, processes, infrastructure, and governance. This approach is sometimes called total assimilation because the target company's way of doing business is typically erased in full integration.

Full integration is much easier to achieve when a more substantial organization absorbs a much smaller company into one of its already existing operating units (sometimes called a tuck-in). Assimilation can also occur when the acquired company becomes a standalone operating unit that relies on the same governance models and infrastructure as the parent (sometimes called a bolt-on).

In the real estate example, our investor buys an apartment building and makes it look like all their other properties. The signage changes, the buildings are painted, the landscaper and other vendors are replaced, and a new team manages the property.

The $4.1 billion acquisition of First Niagara Bank by Key Bank in 2015 took almost a year to complete, but on Columbus Day weekend of 2016, new signs were unveiled and customers were fully transitioned to Key Bank customers[4]. After shuffling various businesses and selling branches to a competitor to satisfy antitrust regulations, the combined bank has increased overall market share, including quadrupling its mortgage business in upstate New York[5].

Much of the success is attributable to Key Bank's customer service culture, which led them to retain over 90 percent of the First Niagara accounts they acquired[6]. Key Bank's HR team was heavily involved in the cultural integration, which included a new onboarding program and culture integration sessions. These efforts were so successful that the bank now delivers the onboarding program they developed for the deal to all new hires and has seen a three percent decrease in voluntary turnover post-merger[7].

Culture clashes are extremely likely to emerge in full assimilation scenarios. Employees from the smaller firm will need to adjust many of the ways they get things done as the larger organization imposes their policies, procedures, processes, and practices.

A Roundtable member shared a full integration deal where the target company's CHRO became the HR director of a newly bolted-on business unit with about 250 employees. The two formed a close relationship as they partnered on the integration and established a regular check in pattern after the employees had made the transition to the acquirer's payroll.

In an effort to minimize culture clash and keep employees happy and productive, the former CHRO frequently asked for exceptions to the acquiring company's IT and HR policies. These exceptions ranged from out-of-cycle promotions to permission to use computers and software that weren't up to IT specifications. At the 18-month mark, they found that nearly 300 exceptions had been requested!

Transform the Business

Business transformation occurs when top executives use a merger or acquisition to reinvent the combined business and make it more competitive. This strategy is most achievable when two organizations of roughly the same size come together. Business leaders can use the infusion of new people, products, and technology to help drive the desired change.

Returning to our real estate scenario, the investor already owns an apartment building and decides to buy another one. The investor picks the best parts of each property's operational management approach, choosing the best manager and vendors for all their buildings, potentially rebranding all of the buildings so they have a consistent look, feel, and renter experience.

Charter Communications' merger with Time Warner Cable and the related acquisition of Bright House Networks moved Charter from the United States' number four cable company to the number two cable provider[8]. When sharing their investor presentation[9] with the market, Charter leadership touted the new combination's 24 million customer relationships and a service network that would touch nearly every state in the union post-merger.

In 2017, Charter announced that they were unifying their pricing and packaging under the new Spectrum cable brand[10]. This transformation took time, as the company wanted to minimize customer disruptions. They took nearly two years to transform the company, a process that included training all maintenance and call center employees on new sales and service systems and standards[11].

While it might not be accurate to refer to the cultural challenges of a business transformation as culture clash, because everybody is changing their ways of working, the cultural pitfalls are significant. Every person involved in the combined company is going through some kind of change, with nobody in the organization feeling stable. Business transformations are a change-management challenge and require thoughtful planning and exceptional change leadership to be successful.

A Roundtable member spent nearly two years working on combining five organizations that had been purchased in short order by a private equity firm. Company leadership took what they saw as the best parts of each organization and asked the entire company to adopt those best-in-class strategies, processes, and tools. While the organization experienced high turnover at the beginning, excellent leaders with strong change acumen were able to rally the employees around the change, increasing the value of the combined firm significantly over the combined purchase prices.

These definitions are general guidelines that might not apply to every scenario. Different organizations have different ways of thinking about their integration models, and HR practitioners are encouraged to check with the business sponsors and corporate development leaders who are making decisions about the future operating model so they can add maximum value through cultural integration.

Chapter 11: Aligning for Successful Culture Change

In an ideal world, the HR practitioner and the integration leader will have ample time to build alignment around the people, leadership, and culture elements of the organizational integration before employees hear about the transaction. This is not often the case, as due diligence, deal negotiations, and gun-jumping regulations make this impractical, especially if the buyer is legally required to announce the final agreement to the market as soon as it's signed.

When it's possible to build alignment before announcement day, the three most critical elements to manage are leadership calibration, organizational design, and total rewards alignment. We should be clear that HR isn't usually responsible for leadership calibration and organizational design but should act as trusted advisors and advocate for these steps to be completed. Total rewards alignment is more typically HR's responsibility but is usually done in collaboration with finance and business leaders who must understand and agree to the financial consequences of any changes.

In cases where the employee announcement day occurs before these elements are managed, the HR practitioner should make sure these activities occur as quickly as practical, since employees will have many questions about the deal and will get understandably anxious if they can't be answered quickly and accurately. We discuss how to handle employee announcement day in Chapter 14.

Leadership Calibration

The most common recommendation in the megamerger literature is a multi-day leadership workshop, where the top managers from each organization come together and discuss the future of the combined company. This is an excellent recommendation for small deals, but the execution must be scaled appropriately for the transactions most HR practitioners will be part of, which will be a somewhat larger company acquiring and integrating an organization with 100 or fewer employees.

Once again, these sessions should be owned by the business sponsor and integration team. HR should participate, and perhaps facilitate, but shouldn't own these sessions as they're designed to ensure the leadership teams from each side of the transaction understand where the combined business is going, both strategically and culturally.

The leadership alignment process often begins prior to the LOI signing, and before HR is even involved, when the business sponsor and corporate development are working with the seller. The conversations often center around how the buyer and target can add value to one another as well as the role of the target company leadership team after the integration is complete. The due diligence process will confirm the buyer's assumptions about the transaction, including financial assumptions. Then, attention usually shifts from due diligence to negotiating the definitive agreement, which can be challenging if there are disagreements around the purchase price or other deal terms.

Once these activities are managed, attention should turn to how the organization will operate post integration. The calibration conversations are likely to begin by defining what success looks like, including the overall strategy, how products and services will be sold, the integration milestones and timelines, and finally how HR matters will be managed.

Calibration conversations are exceptionally important if the seller's compensation includes a holdback or earnout. Holdbacks and earnouts are arrangements where the buyer delays payment of some deal proceeds to key leaders to encourage retention and incentivize sell-side leaders to meet financial, integration, or other milestones that are part of the deal model. Even if the buy-side team isn't thinking about delayed consideration during calibration, the sellers most certainly will be.

The HR practitioner can prepare for this meeting by creating a presentation or document that provides a high-level view of how the employees will be treated during the integration. The impact on employees will vary greatly by integration model. A standalone integration might result in almost no changes, but the target will need to understand any governance requirements they will be expected to follow and understand any additional HR support they can expect after the deal closes.

For partial integrations, full assimilations, and business transformations the changes will be more significant and will require leaders to understand how offers or employment agreements will be handled, including changes to compensation and benefits, general onboarding questions, and how employees who exit either voluntarily or involuntarily will be treated. A high-level overview of the employee communications plan is also helpful, including any talking points the target leadership team will be expected to deliver for smooth integration.

In addition to learning about the employee experience, sell-side leaders want to understand their role in changes to the employee experience, especially any changes in employee total rewards, job titles, reporting structures, and work locations. It is also helpful to preview how the employee lifecycle will be handled once teams are integrated, with emphasis on recruiting, promotions, transfers, and exits.

Each element of the employee lifecycle carries significant risk of culture clash, and many target company leaders are understandably protective of their teams. Setting expectations early can help leaders adjust to the new way of doing things and help them feel better equipped to manage their teams effectively.

Organization Design

An effective organization is one that can deliver on deal value in the context of the integration plan and might require intentional redesign. By their nature, standalone deals usually have limited impact on the organizational structure. Most partial integrations and full assimilations keep the bulk of the target employees in their existing structures, with some back-office departments and employees moving to the buyer's organization. Business transformations frequently require redesigning the entire organization from scratch.

The most common output of the organization design process is an organization chart, with job titles and employee names assigned to each box. Different organizations require different levels of detail as they move through this process, and the HR practitioner will need to use their best judgment as they advise the leaders who are responsible for designing the future organization.

Organization design is another integration planning item where HR can act as an advisor or facilitator but shouldn't be responsible for the overall process. The organizational design work should ultimately be owned by the business sponsor and integration leader, as they will be accountable for deal results.

Layoffs

In some situations, the final organizational design will result in layoffs, which become a symbol of culture clash and can have a significant impact on the morale of remaining employees. If layoffs aren't absolutely necessary, the organization should consider alternatives, like redeploying redundant employees to other parts of the company or absorbing the additional payroll costs until natural attrition right-sizes the business. Employee exits are discussed in more detail in Chapter 19.

Employer of Record

Closely related to organization design are determinations about which legal entity will be the employer of record and how and when employees will transfer between the entities if necessary. In some cases, the acquirer might not be able to make these decisions unilaterally. Collective bargaining agreements, works council consultations, and employee transfer legislation must all be considered as part of this process. Engaging an expert or labor attorney might be necessary to ensure compliance.

Aligning Total Rewards

The final element to consider in cultural integration planning is total rewards, including any changes to base pay, incentives, equity, benefits, and perks, as well as possible alignment of target employees into the buyer's job architecture. Changes to total rewards are most likely to occur in business transformation and full assimilation scenarios.

If the target company remains standalone or is partially integrated, there might not be any planned changes to total rewards. However, there might be implications for the 401(k) controlled group, Affordable Care Act applicable large employer compliance, and the OFCCP single entity test. There might also be implications for pay equity and diversity reporting as regulatory requirements in these areas continue to evolve. The services of a benefits or labor attorney can be helpful in these cases.

To help create a comprehensive picture of total rewards changes and associated cost impacts, many HR practitioners develop a total rewards side-by-side. A total rewards side-by-side allows the HR practitioner to see how the target company's current compensation, benefits, and perks align with the proposed total rewards post-integration.

The HR practitioner might need to create several side-by-sides if the target company has multiple operating units with different total rewards schemes, collective bargaining agreements with specific compensation and benefits provisions, employees in multiple locations, or has different total rewards structures for any other reason. Multiple side-by-sides can also be necessary if employees will be integrated into different acquirer structures.

If an acquisition involves people outside the United States, the HR practitioner will probably need to create a side-by-side for each country where there's an affected employee. Many countries have strict laws governing the treatment of employee total rewards during an M&A event. Compiling the side-by-side can provide an excellent starting point for consultation with an attorney or other expert on transfer legislation in each jurisdiction with employees affected by the deal.

A basic sample total rewards side-by-side template for U.S. operations appears on the next page. HR practitioners will need to modify this template based on the specifics of each deal. A customizable version is part of the Due Diligence Toolkit that can be found on the HR M&A Roundtable website at www.MandARoundtable.com.

Completing the side-by-side requires several decisions with significant financial and cultural impact. As we discussed in Chapter 7, total rewards are a critical part of company culture, and drive a particular set of employee behaviors. Ensuring that the proposed total rewards structure balances company financial needs with incentivizing team and individual performance is one of the most fundamental ways to affect culture change.

Sample Total Rewards Side-by-Side Template for US Operations

Area	Acquirer	Target	Cost Impact	Comments & Recommendations
Annual Payroll				
Base Pay				
Pay Increases				
Performance Management				
Incentive Plans				
Other Bonus Plans				
Equity Granting				
Employee Stock Purchase Plans				
Employee Stock Option Plans				
Medical Plans				
Dental Plans				
Vision Plans				
Flexible Spending Accounts				
Wellness Programs				
Employee Assistance Program				
Pensions				
Retirement Plans				
Life Insurance				
Disability Insurance				
Other Insurances				
Holidays				
Paid Time Off				
Paid and Unpaid Leaves				
Sabbatical				
Other Time Off Programs				
Company Cars				
Paid Parking				
Meals and Snacks				
Gym Memberships				
Pet Insurance				
Legal Insurance				
Financial Planning				
Work-Life Balance Perks				
Career Development Perks				
Other Perks				
Severance Plans				

Chapter 11: Aligning for Successful Culture Change

Calibrating leaders, designing the future organization, and creating total rewards structures are essential to effective cultural integration and should be started as early as possible in the integration process. When possible, completing these steps prior to the employee announcement day will reduce employee stress, driving retention and reducing culture clash. If these steps can't be done before announcement, HR should partner with the business sponsor and integration leader to complete them as soon as possible after employees learn about the deal.

Part 5: Shaping the Acquired Employee Experience

Up to this point, we've focused on the things that happen behind the scenes. We've discussed M&A strategies and processes, the nature, causes and consequences of culture clash, and ways to identify potential problems during due diligence. We've also discussed some ways to partner with business leaders, corporate development, and the integration team to avoid common cultural pitfalls.

Rank-and-file employees and the firm's top leadership will experience the M&A in very different ways. The top leadership team is almost always aware of the sale, and in many cases, they're making key decisions and negotiating the final agreements. Top leaders usually receive significant payouts when the firm sells and are given a level of white glove service that rank-and-file employees do not enjoy during the integration process.

Simply put, the firm's top leaders are in the driver's seat, whereas the typical employee is a passenger. While changing road conditions can be challenging for anybody, twists and turns are often much more difficult for a back-seat passenger who can't predict where the road will change, can't see the potholes and speed bumps, and has no choice but to trust the driver will get them wherever they're going relatively unscathed.

Remember, company culture is *how people get things done in the workplace.* Most of the people getting those things done are the rank-and-file workers, and how they handle the changes to the way things get done will ultimately determine the acquisition's success or failure. In Part 5, we discuss what's going on in employees' heads as they go through the deal lifecycle, ways to plan employee communications, and leading practices for employee announcement day.

Chapter 12: Acquired Employee Psychology

Even though the focus of this book is cultural integration, it's important for HR practitioners to understand that employees can't focus on changing how things get done in the workplace until they've made peace with what is happening to them.

When an employee learns they're being acquired, their world is often turned upside down. A flood of questions enters their mind, and they're caught up in a tangle of conflicting feelings. Two of the most prominent experiences are stress related to uncertainty and an identity crisis.

Maslow's Hierarchy

Both uncertainty and identity are addressed in Maslow's hierarchy of needs[1]. Maslow's hierarchy is usually shown as a pyramid, with the most basic needs at the bottom and more transcendent needs at the top. In this hierarchy, people prioritize their more basic needs first, generally only addressing higher issues on the pyramid when they feel confident that the lower-level needs are being met effectively.

The base of Maslow's pyramid is physiological needs like food, water, shelter, and warmth. Once their physiological needs are met, a person can focus on safety needs, which include physical, emotional, and financial safety. In our society, most people use wages to buy food and pay for housing, meeting their physiological needs via their paycheck. In the United States and many developing countries healthcare is tied to one's job, making work an existential necessity.

Any threat to a person's job security, including an acquisition announcement, will force the employee to confront how their basic needs are met. Until they feel certain in their ability to get food, shelter, clothing, and medical care, acquired employees will have no investment in your strategies and synergy plans.

The next section of Maslow's pyramid deals with psychological needs. Humans are social creatures who require belonging and love to thrive. Most people spend more waking hours with their coworkers than any other group of people in their life, including their families[2]. People start to befriend their coworkers and use their jobs and teams to provide at least part of their social identity.

Once a person feels like they belong in the workplace, they can start to focus on their need for accomplishment alongside the respect and prestige that go with doing important work. Even employees who feel high levels of job security and know their social circles will go unshaken—which is what happens in most standalone acquisitions—still need to reevaluate how they can at least maintain the same level of status and standing when ownership changes. These ingredients combine to create an identity crisis.

Uncertainty Changes Employee Behavior

One of the reasons human beings became the dominant form of life on the planet is our ability to predict threats and then react accordingly. Our ancient ancestors lived in a world with different kinds of dangers than we do. Defending themselves with only their bodies and simple weapons, they had to be constantly aware of large creatures with claws and fangs. Who was going to become whose next meal was often unclear when a person encountered a larger animal!

Imagine a hunter walking through a dense forest with a brace of rabbits that will give the family much needed protein to survive the cold winter. The trees start to rustle, a branch suddenly cracks, and the hunter's heart starts to pound. The adrenaline starts to pump, hearing and vision become more acute, and our hunter starts to run away from the noise. Then another branch snaps, followed by another!

The next few branches snap in front of the hunter, and that's when he realizes that the wind has simply knocked a few loose bits of tree to the ground. There is no mountain lion ready to take his family's dinner, just a stiff breeze making a lot of noise. Our hunter might feel a little foolish or embarrassed, but at least he's alive.

Acquired employees will do the same kind of survival math as our hunter. They'll be hypersensitive to environmental clues and speculate about what's going to happen with their jobs and families. They'll share this information with trusted sources, who will share their own information and speculation in return.

Faced with a lack of certainty, employees will plan for the worst-case scenario – immediate lack of employment. Some will temper concerns about being fired with a wait and see approach, while others will immediately activate their network and begin looking for jobs.

Until there is certainty about their financial and professional future, employees will be distracted and less productive. They'll be more likely to act brashly, grasping for things they hope will provide the psychological certainty they need. Only after they feel secure in their ability to provide food and shelter will they be able to think about anything else.

Identity Changes During M&A

The second major psychological challenge that HR practitioners and the leaders we support must address during M&A is the change to an employee's identity brought about by the acquisition announcement.

Think about the last party you went to and try to recall the number of times you were asked what you do for a living or where you work. Knowing somebody's occupation and employer provides important information about that person not only for the person asking the question, but also the person answering it. Whether we like it or not, where we work is an essential part of our modern identity.

When an acquisition threatens a person's ability to answer those popular party questions and challenges the stability of their coworker relationships, an identity crisis begins to brew. The employee wonders, "Who am I now?" Until that question is answered, employees won't be able to focus on changing their ways of working, prolonging and exacerbating the default culture clash that occurs when two companies combine.

Helping employees overcome their acquisition-related identity crisis requires encouraging them to embrace a new identity as a member of the acquiring organization. This process can be summed up as re-recruitment.

When an employee comes through a traditional hiring route, the recruiter, hiring manager, interviewers, and other members of the hiring team are not only working to assess the candidate's ability to do the work, but they're also helping the employee feel like they would fit in well with the company's culture and existing team members.

The re-recruiting process is similar and requires the buy-side team to work just as hard helping employees see themselves as a good fit in the combined organization. Every interaction matters to the acquired employees, who are usually making career decisions during this critical period. Re-recruiting employees is a must if they're going to move past the identity crisis and choose to remain after the deal closes.

Employee Experience through the Deal Lifecycle

As we discuss the typical employee's experience during M&A, it's helpful to revisit the M&A deal lifecycle, shown below. At each deal phase, employees will experience differing levels of identity crisis and uncertainty[3]. Until they can feel certain about their future employment and their new identity is set, they won't be able to give their full attention to making the deal successful.

Buying A House

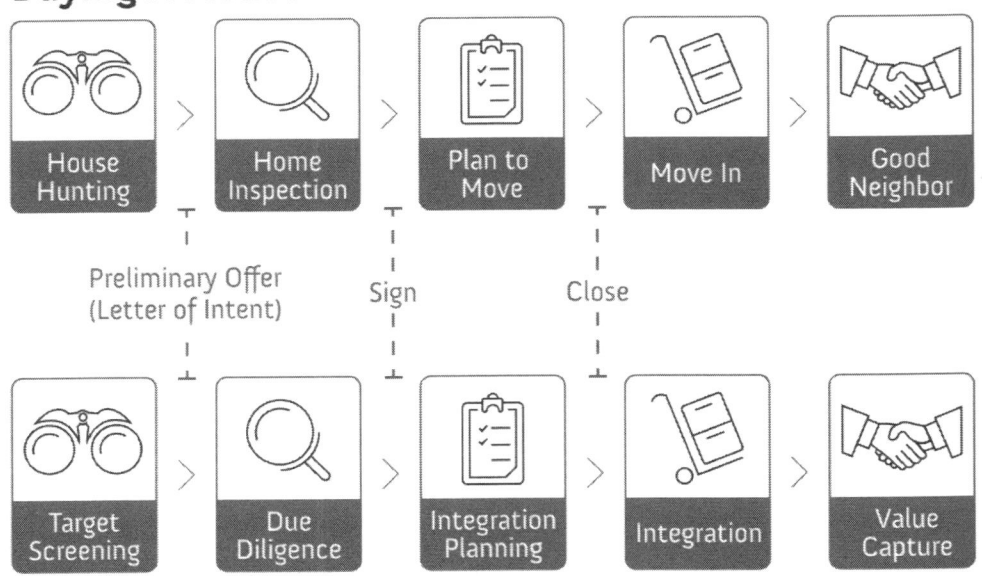

House Hunting > Home Inspection > Plan to Move > Move In > Good Neighbor

Preliminary Offer (Letter of Intent) | Sign | Close

Target Screening > Due Diligence > Integration Planning > Integration > Value Capture

Buying A Company

Chapter 12: Acquired Employee Psychology

Target Screening and Due Diligence

The first two phases of the deal lifecycle are often highly confidential, with only a select few employees aware that the firm might be sold. It's reasonable to assume most employees are unaware of the possible transaction, but employees are more perceptive than many leaders give them credit for.

Leader behavior often changes when a firm is put up for sale. Key leaders typically meet more frequently, becoming less available to employees. They make strange requests for documents and project status. Their stress levels are typically quite high, especially during formal due diligence. When site visits occur, they're usually odd, not feeling quite the same as sales calls or vendor visits.

One IT professional who has been through three acquisitions in her career told me, "We never knew exactly what was happening, but we knew *something* was happening."

In this period, rumors begin to build as employees try to make sense of why their leaders are being so strange. Speculation flies and employees begin to feel uneasy about their future. Uncertainty begins to set in, and employees become distracted from their work because no matter how committed they are to the firm, their primary commitment will be to themselves and their families.

Employee Announcement Day

In many cases, the deal will be announced to employees and the market shortly after the deal is signed. The rumors and information leaks can finally stop now that employees know why their leaders have been behaving so oddly. Unfortunately, that's not the case at all. Instead of breathing a collective sigh of relief, employees experience even more uncertainty as they try to understand what's going on in their world.

A well-managed employee announcement day, which we discuss in Chapter 14, will give employees some certainty and a sense of identity, and is the beginning of the re-recruiting process.

Integration Planning

During the integration planning stage, firms often announce high level changes to the organization. These plans will vary based on the integration plan, but frequently include any changes that will be made to the organization's leadership and structure.

As changes are announced, acquirers should use employee listening techniques (covered in Part 6) to help understand what questions and concerns employees have at both the individual and collective level. Leaders should strive to answer these questions quickly and transparently. The rumors that started during due diligence will only grow stronger as employees try to understand what's going on and prepare themselves for the worst-case scenario.

Employees are actively making decisions about their careers during the integration planning process, making it critical to focus on re-recruiting team members if the deal is going to return value.

Integration

Once the deal closes and the buyer is handed the metaphoric keys to the house, integration begins in earnest, with most companies working on a 100-day plan to transition the business and its most critical processes. During this period, employees experience a takeover as members of the two companies start to interact inside the new culture. The cultural shift becomes more pronounced in integrations based on full assimilation and business transformation, though it's often apparent even when a business is left standalone or only partially integrated.

In some cases, roles, tasks, managers, and work locations are changed. The acquirer introduces new policies, procedures, processes, and practices. New working norms and cultural expectations are taught to the employees, who are grappling with learning how to effectively operate in their new reality.

What's more frustrating to many employees is these changes are being imposed on them due to the acquisition. Unlike their leaders, they didn't ask for the company to be sold and they're not making significant money from the deal. Instead, they're learning how to do a new job that they didn't apply for, with a company they might or might not like, and in a job they might or might not want in the first place.

Further complicating integration is the fact that employees have come over simultaneously. An employee who is hired in a more traditional fashion often comes into a group surrounded by people who know how to get things done in the organization and they just need to ask for help to acculturate. An acquired employee doesn't have access to that kind of social support. Something as simple as booking a business trip can be nightmarish if nobody understands the rules and there's no one available to help navigate the travel and expense system.

During integration, the employee feels the least in-control and might believe that exiting the organization gives the best chance of experiencing the sense of certainty that comes from being in control of one's own destiny. It's important to continue employee listening and re-recruitment efforts during this initial integration period.

Value Capture

Once the most significant changes have been made, usually around the 100-day mark, the organization begins to stabilize. Employees feel more certain about their work situation and new social bonds begin to form. Changes might still happen, but they feel more predictable and less significant than the massive changes that result from the announcement and subsequent integration. Roles, tasks, and reporting structures start to solidify, and the new policies, procedures, processes, and practices start to feel familiar. Employees know their place in the company and are better able to manage the additional changes that come with any job. In short, things start to feel normal.

Employee Reactions Have Financial Consequences

While employees have many different psychological reactions to an M&A deal, uncertainty and the identity crisis are the most significant to consider for preserving deal value. Managing them carefully isn't just a matter of empathizing with people going through a significant life event, it's also about preserving deal value.

When the work environment becomes uncertain, employees look for stability. For many of them, that means changing employers. Several studies have found acquired employee attrition is at least twice[4] that of traditional hires, with some studies finding the number to be far greater.

At the leadership level the picture is the same. A longitudinal study of 23,000 executives in 1,000 target firms found that leadership attrition in merged firms is more than double that of comparable enterprises. Even more concerning, this effect can last up to a decade post-merger[5]!

Turnover can also be contagious. The departure of one influential employee can start a domino effect, with other employees quickly following suit. For many acquired employees, the departure of their coworkers only aggravates their uncertainty and identity crisis.

Many companies use retention packages to incentivize employees to stay, but these incentives aren't always effective. Sometimes no amount of money makes up for being miserable at work. Furthermore, a sufficiently motivated competitor will pay a sign-on bonus to cover the loss of the retention incentive. Relying solely on financial incentives is not likely to be effective for the most talented team members.

When most employees leave, deal value walks out the door with them. In addition to the hard costs of hiring and retraining replacements, the firm must deal with lower productivity while the role is vacant and during the training period. Customer service standards can slip, vendor relationships can become mismanaged, and sales teams can take lucrative revenue streams with them. As we saw during the Great Resignation that started in 2021, if enough employees leave, a business might have no choice but to shut down.

Even if employees stay with the organization, there will likely be a noticeable productivity dip as both total employee output and work quality drops because employees are distracted by the changes happening in their work environment. While a slowdown is almost inevitable during a period of massive change, properly handling the employee experience can make this period go by more quickly and minimize the drop in output, creating less risk to the business than a deep and prolonged productivity dip.

It's in the best financial interests of a company to manage the integration properly, leading employees through the culture clash, uncertainty-related stress, and identity crisis as effectively as possible.

Chapter 13: Employee Communications

The most effective tools for overcoming culture clash and addressing both uncertainty-related stress and the identity crisis are rooted in communication. As we saw in Chapter 12, in the absence of clear, credible information, employees will create a worst-case-scenario story that makes sense to them and react accordingly.

To help avoid the financial consequences that follow mass resignations and the productivity dip that follows major change, organizations must have an effective employee communications plan that focuses on both culture change and re-recruitment.

The overarching goals for employee communications include helping employees understand why the acquisition is happening and ensuring they continue to provide high-quality products and services to their customers. The goal of operational continuity is served when communications focus on re-recruitment, helping to maintain morale, drive retention, and facilitate smooth cultural integration over the course of the integration planning and integration phases.

The employee communications plan is only one part of an overarching effort to let all affected stakeholders know about the transaction and how it will affect them. The integration leader will usually coordinate a broader communication workstream that includes communications professionals and members of the sales, marketing, and supplier management teams. In addition, business leaders are often the ones delivering key messages to employees. For this reason, HR shouldn't own the overall communications plan, but act as a key member of a larger team working to ensure stakeholders get the right information at the right time.

Each deal's key messages will vary depending on the nature and needs of the specific transaction. Not every key message should be shared at once, as this will overwhelm most employees. An effective communications plan ensures the right people get the right information, from the right person, at the right time.

This chapter will cover the basics of effective acquired employee communications, but the HR practitioner will need to adjust the plan to fit the specific circumstances of their deal, including what they discover during cultural due diligence.

Develop Key Messages

Most integration processes involve a staggering amount of information, making it necessary to distill the list to a manageable number of key messages. Key messages often include the strategic reasons for the acquisition, changes to the leadership team, how the firms will integrate, how employee selection occurred or will occur, changes to total rewards, and changes to policies and practices.

In addition, the integration team needs to develop key messages that focus on re-recruitment, reminding employees why they should choose to stay on after the deal closes. These messages should be based on the buy-side employee value proposition and can be informed by looking at the messaging the acquirer draws on to attract and hire people using traditional methods. Typical re-recruitment messages are employee-focused and include enhanced total rewards, opportunities for professional development, and future growth trajectories.

Finally, some key messages will center on the changes happening to the organization. To ensure employees understand and can personalize important information, each key change message should incorporate the following four elements:

- The thing that will change
- How and when the change will occur
- How the change will affect employees
- How the company will help employees through the change

Because the employee communications plan is designed to provide certainty, re-recruit and provide a new identity, craft the key messages to avoid using us/them language. It's also helpful to refer to acquired employees as new colleagues or new team members—rather than by their old company name—as quickly as deal conditions permit.

Understand the Audience

While it's tempting to view every employee in an acquired organization as the audience for every key message the acquirer needs to deliver, it can quickly become overwhelming for employees to focus on every bit of information associated with a deal.

Some messages will be applicable to an entire organization, but even small organizations usually have employee groups with different concerns and communication needs. For example, people who work in different locations, including those who work in different countries or in fully remote jobs, will have different needs from those who work at a headquarters location. Other key audience segments include line managers, exiting employees, and members of specific functions or departments.

Line Managers

Line managers often have the most challenging role in any M&A deal. They're usually too far down the organization's hierarchy to know about the deal, leaving them to manage their own uncertainty-related stress and identity crisis. They then have the additional burden of concurrently helping their team members navigate their new reality.

In many cases, acquirers rely on line managers to help cascade information to employees. A person's line manager is often their most trusted messenger[1] and is critical to both communications and re-recruitment efforts. Preparing line managers for their dual role is critical to deal success.

Exiting Employees

Employees who will leave the organization have their own unique communication needs, whether or not they leave of their own accord. Employees who exit voluntarily need to understand offboarding expectations and timelines, including who to contact with questions. Those who are going to be laid off also need to understand whether they can find another job in the organization, along with any severance, medical coverage, and unemployment benefits they might be eligible to receive.

How an acquirer treats exiting employees reflects their culture and will be noticed by employees who stay with the firm. Respectful treatment that includes clear communications makes a difference in driving deal value.

Functions and Departments

Some messages are only applicable to people in specific functions or departments. For example, HR doesn't need to know about changes to the press release format and the marketing team doesn't need to understand that there's a new form for employee onboarding. Similarly, while all employees should be told about changes to the organizational structure, those who are directly impacted by a new leader or team structure will have more detailed questions that need to be answered.

Buy-Side Employees

While the focus of this book is on acquired employees, it's also important to think about how employees on the buy side might react to the acquisition and ensure they're considered in the overall communications plan.

Identify the Messengers

Once the HR practitioner understands the key messages and the appropriate audience for each one, they must decide who should deliver each message and the best way to ensure employees receive the information they need.

The most effective messengers are those who are trusted by the audience and can deliver the necessary information in a way that connects with the employees' heads and hearts. For employees to trust the information—earning their heads—messages must be delivered clearly, using language the employees understand. Sharing facts, data, and visuals can be helpful.

For employees to trust the messenger—earning their hearts—the messenger must show empathy and respect for the acquired firm's culture and understand that employees are going through a difficult time caused by uncertainty and the identity crisis. The old adage rings true here, people don't care how much you know until they know how much you care.

Some key messages will require multiple messengers, each reinforcing a key point. In this instance, it's critical to have each messenger repeating the key messages in the same way to avoid exacerbating employee uncertainty.

Other messages will be communicated without attributing the message to any individual, like those that are shared via a group email or posted to an integration portal. Even when there's no single messenger, it's important to let employees know who to turn to for questions.

Choose the Medium

Once you know who will be delivering which key messages, the next step is choosing how the messages will be delivered to employees. Two common forms of broad-based communications during M&A are town hall meetings and frequently asked questions (FAQ) documents.

Town hall style meetings allow a significant number of employees to hear the same messages at the same time. They're typically agenda-driven, with different speakers sharing the key messages where they're the most appropriate messenger. These meetings are often recorded so employees can review the information later if necessary. The employee announcement meeting (covered in Chapter 14) is usually a town hall meeting.

Frequently asked questions (FAQs) documents allow the integration team and HR practitioner to consider the most urgent and important questions the employees might have and share a consistent set of responses. These documents are often the backbone of a strong employee communications plan because they answer the personal questions employees will focus on first, including those around job security and changes to total rewards.

Some leaders share emails or video recordings, and others like to share on Slack or the company intranet site. Still others like to share messages in less formal ways. The HR practitioner most likely learned about the organization's communication styles and preferences during cultural due diligence and further solidified their understanding as they worked with leaders during integration planning. An understanding of those communication preferences should shape the final plan.

Set the Schedule

Once the integration team knows what (key messages), who (trusted messengers), and how (media) employee communications will be managed, they can focus on when the messages will be delivered to each audience.

The most effective communications are timely and predictable. Messages need to be scheduled so they go out when employees need the information. If messages are sent out too early, they can potentially overwhelm employees with too much information. The most effective timing of messages depends a great deal on the acquired company's culture. Consultation with the integration team and acquired leaders will help ensure the messaging schedule is as effective as possible.

Update as Needed

Finally, the communications plan can't be a static document where pre-written messages are automatically sent on a pre-determined cadence. All elements of the plan must be continuously monitored to ensure employee's ever-changing needs are being met. The communications plan should be responsive to the employee listening strategy, which is covered in Part 6.

A well planned and executed communications strategy helps ensure employees understand why the acquisition is happening and can focus on providing high-quality products and services to their customers. It provides certainty, re-recruits employees, and invites a new identity, minimizing the disruptions that create culture clashes, attrition, and a productivity dip, thereby preserving deal value.

Chapter 14: Employee Announcement Day

Learning about an acquisition is a pivotal moment in an employee's career. Even if employees suspect the deal is happening, the announcement makes it real. Employee announcement day is the acquirer's chance to make an excellent first impression.

The psychological importance of employee announcement day is well known in M&A circles, and for most serial acquirers it kicks off a 100-day period of intense integration activity that includes frequent employee communications (Chapter 13), employee listening (Part 6), and other onboarding and cultural integration activities (Part 7).

The Manager Meeting

As we discussed in Chapter 13, line managers have a twofold challenge during the integration process. In addition to managing their own uncertainty and identity crisis, managers are responsible for leading team members who are having similar reactions to the deal. Hosting a manager meeting immediately before the employee town hall is a leading practice for equipping line managers to handle the challenges ahead of them.

The first items on the manager meeting agenda mirror the first several items covered during the employee town hall, which we discuss next. The meeting should start with the acquired leader announcing the acquisition, reinforcing the importance of keeping the information confidential until it can be shared with employees. Next, top leaders should handle the three big questions line managers will have about their own careers, followed by a brief overview of the deal. All of these items are covered in the section on the employee town hall.

After line managers understand the deal and how it will affect them personally, they should be trained on common employee reactions to an acquisition announcement and how they should manage any questions or behavioral issues that might arise. Finally, they should be given a list of resources that will help them lead both themselves and their teams through the change. The meeting should end with Q&A and be timed so the managers move from their own meeting directly into the employee town hall to minimize the chances of information leaking.

The Announcement Town Hall

The most common way to let employees know about an M&A deal is an employee town hall. In this format, the employees come together either in person or virtually to hear from their leaders. Some of them will know about the acquisition, and many of them will suspect it. All of them will know something big has happened.

Announce the Acquisition

Employees want to know what's going on, so sell-side leaders should start the meeting by announcing the acquisition. This should be a short, quick message that shares who the buyer is and why the deal was done.

Once the basic deal announcement is made, the sell-side leader introduces the buy-side business leader and any members of the deal team they'd like the employees to meet. The buy-side leader should start by sharing their excitement about the acquisition and thank the sell-side leaders for the partnership they've had so far. They can then briefly speak about their hopes and high-level plans for the combined company.

It's critically important that the initial announcement be focused on the employees and doesn't become a victory lap for the buy-side deal team. The introductions should be brief and sensitive to the uncertainty and identity crisis that most employees are suddenly confronted with. The employees' needs must be attended to quickly, and a protracted strategy conversation doesn't set the right tone.

One challenging announcement meeting I was part of started with an excited and well-intentioned corporate development leader spending six minutes detailing how the transaction started and the process for getting it done, seemingly unaware that the employees' attention was elsewhere.

The employee feedback was less than flattering. The tone-deaf introduction damaged employee morale. The sell-side leadership team took several weeks reassuring their team members and building employee trust in the buying organization. It made the re-recruitment process much more difficult, delaying cultural integration. There is a time for leaders to discuss specifics of the transaction, but that time isn't the beginning of the announcement meeting.

Answer the Three Big Questions

After a brief announcement, focus should shift from the transaction to the employees. When employees learn about an acquisition, three major questions immediately come to the front of their mind. As we covered in our discussion of Maslow's pyramid (see Chapter 12), the employee's physiological and safety needs must be addressed before the employee can focus on anything else, including the buyer, the strategy, or the specifics of the transaction.

The three big questions are:
- Do I still have a job?
- Will you be fair to me?
- Will my job be as good?

Imagine yourself in the employee's seat. You've just found out that your employer has been bought. The thoughts running through your mind include *What am I going to tell my spouse? What if I get fired? Do I have enough in savings to make it until I find another job? How will they decide who gets to keep their job? What's going to happen with my health insurance? Do I still get a retirement match?*

These questions are very personal and have to do with the employee's ability to provide food, clothing, shelter, and medical attention for themselves and the most important people in their lives. Answer the three big questions first.

What's not running through an employee's mind right away are questions like: *Why did they buy us in the first place? What's the new go-to-market strategy? How will they consolidate our service offerings? What does the new org chart look like?* There's a place for those questions later, but until the three big questions are answered, most employees simply don't care about the deal strategy and can't focus on the integration work required to create deal value.

Do I still have a job?

Job security is the most important issue on every employee's mind following an acquisition announcement. Much of the uncertainty felt during M&A deals is driven by this question and employees won't be able to focus on anything else until they have a believable answer to this question.

If there won't be layoffs, let the employees know. However, be sure this is the right answer, because if there are layoffs later in the deal lifecycle, employees will feel lied to and morale will plummet, leading to increased attrition that can destroy deal value.

If there will be layoffs, say so and describe the process that will be used to decide who stays and who goes. Assure the employees that the buyer will be as fair as possible and let them know what kind of severance, insurance continuation, outplacement services, and other support will be available for terminated employees.

If the buyer is unsure about layoffs, that should be shared as well, along with the process and timeline for making that determination.

Will you be fair to me?

Acquired employees are unlikely to ask this question directly, but fairness concerns are top of mind. The employees are being asked to trust that the buyer will treat them fairly and respectfully, while they can't help but plan for the worst-case scenario. This conflict drives a great deal of the uncertainty-related stress employees must overcome to be productive during the upcoming months.

The best way to start earning employee trust, and help them feel more certain about their future, is to explain both the rationale and process for decisions that affect them on a personal level. The key points for change messages are an excellent way to reinforce the buyer's commitment to treating employees fairly. Those four messaging elements are:
- The thing that will change
- How and when the change will occur
- How the change will affect employees
- How the company will help employees through the change

Chapter 14: Employee Announcement Day

Will my job be as good?

In addition to answering a question that's top of mind for most of the acquired team, answering this question allows the buyer to start re-recruiting employees. Employees naturally want to identify with an excellent employer and as part of a high-performing team. Use the announcement meeting to tell them what makes the company and team exceptional and get them excited by the opportunity to move from one great company to another great company.

In addition to the acquirer's reputation, what makes a job good varies by employee, but at the very least this question points to pay, benefits, job titles, and job descriptions. Any known changes to these factors should be shared up front, along with the process that was used to reach these decisions. If decisions are yet to be made, explain how the process works and how sell-side leaders are involved in the decision-making process.

Share Details of the Deal and Integration

Once employees know what will happen with their personal circumstances, they can start to think about other parts of the deal. At this point in the town hall, it's appropriate to talk about the high-level deal rationale and timeline. The focus should remain on how the transaction affects employees and their stakeholders, including coworkers, customers, and vendors.

The talking points in this section of the meeting can start to focus on cultural items, including the expected integration model, changes to company leadership, and updates to the organization structure. These points should remain high level, as details tend to be fluid during these early stages. Avoiding detailed commitments makes it easier to change the plan when the integration team has more information.

During cultural due diligence, the deal team analyzed the deal-specific considerations of strategy, synergies, and sacred cows. Any high-level changes to these three areas can also be discussed in this part of the town hall along with any significant changes to critical policies, procedures, and practices that the integration team believes should be communicated at this point.

Finally, give employees a sense of the 100-day plan and the major milestones they'll experience. Not all milestones will be applicable in all deals, but employees need to know about the events that will impact them directly. Significant events are detailed in Part 7, and include receiving employment offers, changes to pay and benefits, transfers from one payroll to another, policy and process updates, location moves, buddy programs, and so on.

Manage Employee Q&A

Employees will have several questions about the transaction, but they might not ask those questions during the town hall, depending on the company culture and individual reactions. When preparing for the town hall, the HR practitioner, integration team, and sell-side leaders should spend a few minutes anticipating the kinds of questions the employees will have. Then, a few members of the sell-side leadership team should come to the town hall with pre-arranged questions for the buy-side speakers. Not only does this ensure the most critical questions get answered, but it also gets the conversation started and helps employees know that asking questions is appropriate and encouraged.

Questions should be answered as truthfully as possible. If an answer is uncertain, say so. It's better to tell an employee, "I don't know" than it is to share inaccurate information. Once an employee feels lied to by a leader, it's almost impossible to regain their trust.

Finally, never say, "nothing will change." This is simply not the case. Something has already changed because somebody else is ultimately in charge of the organization. Employees are expecting things to be different and telling them nothing will change feels inauthentic, making a statement designed to provide comfort feel like a bald-faced lie.

Offer Corporate Swag

One of the most effective ways to lead employees through the identity crisis is to offer them a new identity to grab onto. An inexpensive way to do that is the use of corporate swag. Popular swag includes office supplies like mousepads and sticky notes, mugs and reusable cups, and

Chapter 14: Employee Announcement Day

tech items like chargers and speakers. If the buyer is a manufacturer or distributor, giving away product employees might use can be great swag.

T-shirts can be very effective and give employees a way to literally wear their new affiliation. I once attended an employee announcement day where word of the acquisition had leaked, and nearly 80 percent of the employees came to the town hall dressed in the seller's logo items in a show of solidarity.

Seeing this, and understanding he needed to lead the way for his team, the founder asked me for one of the new t-shirts we had brought and put it on the podium. He announced the deal, introduced the business sponsor, and shared how excited he was for the company's future. He then took the t-shirt and put it on over his dress shirt, setting an example for his team by embracing the new identity.

He then helped the integration team hand out the new shirts before the meeting continued, further expressing his excitement about being a member of a new team made up of both the buyer and seller. While not every employee put the new shirt on right away, many followed his example and did. The leader's quick thinking and decisive action led his team through the first steps of their identity change in a way that respected the employees and culture.

Announcement Day Celebration Event

Many acquirers host an announcement day event to celebrate the acquisition. These celebrations can be an important way for the acquired employees to feel like part of the new team, both as a re-recruitment step and as an important part of moving past the acquisition-induced identity crisis.

These celebrations can also backfire if employees feel like the day is more of a victory lap than an acknowledgment of the transition. Experienced leaders should adjust the tone of the announcement day event to reflect the tone of the employee town hall. If the mood is upbeat, then cheerful music and colorful balloons might be the perfect way to build employee goodwill. But if the mood is somber, then those same balloons and happy tunes will be too stark a contrast and are likely to exacerbate hard feelings. Read the room and plan to be flexible if you host a celebration event.

The acquired leadership team should be front and center of any announcement day celebration event. Their knowledge of the employee base will help ensure the event strikes the right tone, and their active leadership in the event sends a strong message that they respect the buyer and trust them to do the right things.

Leader and HR Office Hours

The final element of the employee announcement day consists of both leader and HR office hours. Handling integration meetings and analyst or press interviews are an important part of a leader's job, but the most successful leaders balance these obligations with their responsibilities to the people who will soon become the newest members of their teams. One of the easiest ways for buy-side leaders to be visible and accessible is holding office hours. This practice is recommended for the business sponsor, integration lead, HR leader, and anybody else who was visible during the announcement meeting.

Office hours are easy to coordinate. All it takes is an office and a little bit of time. The leader sits in the office during their designated block of time and waits for employees to come with introductions, questions, or concerns and then handles them appropriately.

It's not uncommon for business leaders to set aside 90 minutes to meet with acquired employees and yet nobody comes to visit. While this might feel like a failure, it sends an important message to the acquired employees, and they notice that the leader is taking time from their busy day to spend with their newest team members.

If an HR practitioner or leader wants to earn bonus points with employees, they should take time to walk around employee areas, assuming conditions permit in-person interactions. Making the effort to approach employees and soliciting questions goes a long way toward showing acquired employees how much the buy-side team cares.

In most cases, there's a period between the deal being announced and the deal closing. During this period, the integration team and HR can continue to work on the integration plan, including refining the alignment work discussed in Chapter 11. It's also the time to kick off employee listening, which is the next topic in this book

Part 6: Employee Listening

During the due diligence phase, HR practitioners have very little access to the target company's employee population, requiring the use of proxies to gather important cultural intelligence. In Part 3's discussion of cultural due diligence, we focused on ways to learn about the target company's culture using publicly available sources, documents gathered during due diligence, and contact with the target company's leadership team.

During cultural due diligence, the M&A team makes a series of educated assumptions about employee sentiment, however these information sources can be incredibly biased. Anonymous social media sites like Glassdoor and Yelp tend to skew toward extremes, as people who are deeply in love with the firm and those with an axe to grind are more likely to leave feedback than those with neutral sentiment[1].

Similarly, sell-side leaders are often unreliable. These leaders have an understandable desire to maximize purchase price, which will increase their personal wealth. They do this by casting their organization in the most positive light possible. An HR M&A Roundtable member shared that she's stopped asking leaders if there are any performance issues during due diligence interviews because the answer is always no. "Despite the no's," she continued, "it seems like I'm always being asked how to terminate a problem employee within a few days of closing the deal."

Leaders on both sides are likely to be "out of touch with employees and need a wake-up call[2]," as Microsoft's 2021 Work Trend Index boldly asserts. The disconnect occurs because leaders are often in different demographic groups, have more autonomy, earn more money, and enjoy superior work-life balance compared to employees. Furthermore, leaders create the culture in which employees operate, giving them a strong reason to embrace their ways of working, which might or might not be ideal for the employee base.

This is not to say leaders are inherently dishonest or ill-intentioned. In fact, leaders can be a key source of cultural information, but they're, like all of us, complex human beings with strengths, weaknesses, and blind spots that HR practitioners should account for when discussing important drivers of deal value.

Relying on review sites and leader feedback will create a skewed baseline, making it critically important to gather feedback directly from the employees. In this part, we will discuss four common techniques for employee listening during mergers and acquisitions: culture surveys, pulse surveys, focus groups, and stay interviews.

In addition to the structured employee listening opportunities listed above, several other cultural integration techniques provide opportunities to listen. Leader office hours provide a chance to exchange information, and most town hall sessions end with Q&A. Leading acquirers take advantage of these informal listening opportunities.

Before we dive into employee listening techniques, it's important to differentiate hearing from listening. Hearing is a passive process. When we hear, we are simply perceiving sounds. Listening, on the other hand, is active. It requires attention and effort to make meaning of the sounds in our environment.

Since this part is about listening, each chapter concludes with a reminder that the HR practitioner shouldn't ask questions if the acquirer doesn't intend to act on what the employees say. Ignoring employees who have been generous enough to share their thoughts and concerns during an exceptionally vulnerable time in their lives and careers will further demoralize the organization, exacerbating the culture clashes while increasing uncertainty-related stress.

While the emphasis of this section is listening to acquired employees, the HR practitioner should ascertain the need for buy-side employee listening. If the go-forward operating model will shake up the acquiring organization, the firm risks additional uptick in employee resignations and a downtick in productivity and profitability due to the changes experienced by buy-side employees. This makes it important to carefully consider the need for a listening strategy on both sides of the deal.

One important caveat to the timing of employee listening involves concerns around gun-jumping, which occurs when the buyer exercises illegal control over the seller prior to the transaction closing. Be sure to consult an attorney to ensure your employee listening strategy is implemented only when it's legal to do so.

Chapter 15: Pulse Surveys

Pulse surveys are one of the most powerful employee listening tools available during M&A integration. They're like the annual employee engagement surveys that many organizations use because they're designed to measure how the entire workforce feels about their organization and its leaders.

Annual surveys are wide-ranging, including dozens of questions, and typically take 20 to 30 minutes to complete. The annual surveys give employees the chance to confidentially offer feedback to their management team. In an ideal situation, leaders use these surveys to pinpoint areas of both challenge and excellence in the organization. They give leadership critical information about the firm's ability to execute its strategic intent through its people.

Pulse surveys are similar in nature but are intentionally designed to take less than five minutes to complete and focus on only one area – in this case, the integration. The term pulse implies a steady rhythm, and pulse surveys are best delivered on a reliable cadence. Finally, pulse surveys should be customized so they're asking questions that are relevant to employees in the moment.

While it might be tempting to wait several weeks for employees to digest all the information coming out about the merger before launching a survey, delaying employee listening can be a big mistake. Once employees know about the deal, you must assume your competitors and headhunters know about it as well. HR M&A Roundtable Member Dr. Marc Prine summed it up succinctly when he said, "Headhunters are sharks, and an acquisition announcement is blood in the water."

Employees are going to talk to somebody. It's up to you to decide if that somebody is you or one of your competitors. The leading practice is to send your initial pulse survey right after the employee announcement meeting.

Create Meaningful Questions

In addition to the uncertainty-related stress and identity crisis that follow an acquisition announcement, a deal often creates extra work for the affected employees. This is why brief, focused pulse surveys are one of the best techniques for employee listening. Pulse surveys should take less than five minutes to complete, which means they should contain no more than 10 questions, only one or two of which are open-ended.

Survey items should be clear and relevant. Before deploying your survey, step into your audience's shoes and ask 1) is the question easy to understand?, 2) do my employees care about this question?, and 3) will I be able to take action on the responses?. If the answer to any of the questions is "no," consider rewriting or replacing the question with one that's a better fit for your audience.

To make the survey easy to answer, most of the questions should use what survey geeks call a Likert-type scale. This allows employees to rate their level of agreement with each survey question. For shorter surveys, like a pulse survey, there's an advantage to using a 7-point scale, which is why they're used in the samples included in this chapter. Using a 5- or 9-point scale is also acceptable if they work better in your organization's culture.

To make the surveys easier for employees to answer, use the same scale throughout the entire acquisition. If your organization does frequent acquisitions, using the same scale on every deal will allow you to compare results from different transactions.

The best open-ended questions are broad and solicit direct employee feedback. It's not uncommon for employees to leave these sections blank, especially in a low trust environment or when things are going well. That's okay. Keep the open-ended questions in the survey anyway.

Some questions should continue throughout the course of the integration, while others should only be asked when certain change events occur or particular milestones are met. This chapter includes sample questions you can use or modify for your deal and show how some questions should be ongoing and others are event dependent.

Chapter 15: Pulse Surveys

Sample Announcement Day Questions

This section includes some questions to include in the pulse survey that's sent to employees shortly after they learn about the acquisition. As always, HR practitioners should apply their best judgment to the actual questions put in front of employees.

Please rate your level of agreement with each of the following statements related to the acquisition:

1	2	3	4	5	6	7
Strongly Disagree	Disagree	Somewhat Disagree	Neutral	Somewhat Agree	Agree	Strongly Agree

- I feel valued by [acquirer name]
- I understand how the acquisition will affect my role
- I believe the acquisition will be good for my career
- I believe the acquisition will be good for our business
- I understand the reasons for the acquisition
- I believe in [target name]'s ability to successfully make the transition
- I trust the leaders on both sides will take the right steps to make the acquisition successful
- My most important questions were answered during the announcement meeting

Please provide your feedback on the following questions:
- What are your three biggest questions or concerns about the acquisition?
- What is the most important thing we should do to make the acquisition successful?

Sample Follow-on Questions:

The follow-on questions on the next page include several items that can be asked on every survey to ensure employee sentiment is moving in the right direction. Other questions relate to specific change events or integration milestones. Again, HR practitioners should use their best judgment when using questions from this list or creating their own items.

Please rate your level of agreement with each of the following statements related to the acquisition:

1	2	3	4	5	6	7
Strongly Disagree	Disagree	Somewhat Disagree	Neutral	Somewhat Agree	Agree	Strongly Agree

- I feel welcome and valued in the new organization
- I understand how my role contributes to our company's success
- The acquisition has been good for my career
- The acquisition has been good for our business
- I am included in the decisions that affect my work
- My workload has been reasonable following the acquisition
- My team is supportive of the acquisition
- My direct manager is giving me the support I need
- I can easily find the information I need
- I understand the changes to my pay and benefits
- I have had the right training to do my job well
- I can effectively navigate the new systems
- I have enough time to effectively manage both my normal work responsibilities while also managing my transition
- I would recommend our company to a qualified friend who is looking for work
- I see myself working here in two years

Please provide your feedback on the following questions:
- What additional information or resources do you need to be successful in your job?
- What can we do differently to make the integration more successful?

Determine the Survey Cadence

One of the more challenging parts of listening via pulse surveys is deciding how often to ask questions of acquired employees. Many leaders are concerned that the surveys will distract employees from doing their work. Fortunately, pulse surveys are short by design, meaning they won't take much of the team's time. And, let's face it, employees are in the middle of an acquisition integration, so they're already distracted.

Another common concern is survey fatigue. Fortunately, McKinsey research shows that a clear, relevant, useful survey that you intend to act on won't trigger survey fatigue[1]. To be clear – don't send a survey if you aren't going to act on it!

The leading practice is to send pulse surveys when the employees experience a major change event. An obvious change occurs when employees learn about the acquisition, which is why HR practitioners should send a pulse survey within 24 hours of the announcement meeting if conditions permit. Other changes that might warrant a survey include major news coverage of the deal, amendments to integration timelines such as deal delays, adjustments to total rewards, moving to a new company's payroll, shifts in leaders or the organization structure, and so on.

If there's a lengthy period between change events—which might happen if there are long lead times for regulatory approvals or integration is intentionally delayed—a monthly survey tells employees that their thoughts and feelings are still important. Monthly survey results provide important information about what to include in regular employee communications and allows the integration team to track employee sentiment as it changes over time. It also provides time to process the results and communicate back to employees how the integration team has acted on the prior survey.

Invite Participation

Because survey completion should remain voluntary, there are often questions about how integration teams can encourage employees to participate in the pulse surveys. The first step to driving high response rates is creating clear, relevant, and easy-to-understand questions – topics covered earlier in this section. Other important ways to increase participation include leader support, survey accessibility, and timely reminders.

Leader support is one of the easiest and most important ways to drive a high response rate. Clear messaging from both buy- and sell-side leaders tells employees that their thoughts are important to the entire leadership team. Communication should include why employees are being surveyed, who will review the results, and how the leadership team will use what they learn. In addition to selling the value of participation, messaging should reinforce the confidential nature of the survey. Finally, the message should close with a call to action that includes where employees should go to take the survey and the deadline for responding.

In addition to ensuring top leader support, integration teams should equip front line managers with the tools they need to encourage team members to participate. This can be as simple as asking front line leaders to forward emails from top leaders or asking them to mention the survey during their team and one-on-one meetings.

Employees are more likely to respond to a survey when it's easy to get to and easy to complete. If a survey sits behind a firewall or requires a complicated sign on process, response rates will drop. Employees need the opportunity to complete the survey from their work computer or mobile phone. Survey access from a smartphone is especially important for employees who don't have regular access to a work computer, like people working in field sales, food service, touch labor, warehouse, or factory jobs. Deploying the survey so it's accessible for employees with disabilities will also increase response rates.

If your workforce is international or multilingual, employees should be given the opportunity to complete the survey in a language other than English. This might require paying for a professional translator. The acquiring company likely paid millions of dollars for the target, trying to save a few hundred dollars on translation services is a grave error. The acquirer will probably spend more than that replacing employees who reasonably assume a low-quality translation means the buyer doesn't care about their non-English-speaking workforce.

Motivating employees to take part in pulse surveys might be a challenge in some organizations. If the response rates are low, it might indicate a low-trust culture already exists. Employees might not feel like the survey is worth their time to take since they don't believe it will make a difference. Instead of cajoling or bribing more employees to take the survey, understand that choosing to not participate in the survey is a type of response and start working to increase trust among the workforce.

When the response rates are less than expected, some organizations leave surveys open for prolonged periods or continue to extend the deadline for survey completion. In a fast-moving integration, the extensions can be problematic for supporting the survey and follow-up communications cadence. Rather than extend the deadline, use other employee listening tools to gather the information you need. Finally, understand that employees are more motivated to take a survey when they feel like their voice truly matters.

After the Survey

Once the pulse survey closes, the HR practitioner should review the answers and prepare a report to share with the integration and leadership team members. The report should include the raw survey data, including both the net numeric scores of the scaled items and the complete text of any open-ended responses, though some light editing may be required to ensure confidentiality. Next, the report should include analysis of the results and any recommendations for next steps. When the survey results involve other functions, HR should coordinate with those groups to ensure alignment on analysis and recommendations before they're shared with leadership.

If individuals are recognized as being helpful to the integration, HR should acknowledge those individuals in a manner appropriate to the organization's culture. If individuals are called out as being harmful to the integration, HR should also act accordingly.

The integration team should use the survey results to evaluate the re-recruiting efforts and communications plans that were developed using the principles outlined in Chapter 13.

Once leadership has reviewed the responses and aligned on a path forward, high level results should be shared with employees. This can be as simple as sharing the average scores for each question along with a simple summary in a *you said X, we're doing Y* format. This lets employees know that they've been heard. It will also increase response rates for the next survey administration.

Like all employee listening, pulse surveys can be an effective way to understand what's going on with the employees. However, employee engagement can plummet if the integration team doesn't act on the information they've collected. If you aren't committed to listening to the employees and taking action, don't do pulse surveys!

Chapter 16: Culture Surveys

Many organizations use the term *cultural assessment* when referring to a culture survey that's deployed to the target employee population. This book avoids applying that language to culture surveys since true assessment of the culture begins at target screening and continues throughout the deal lifecycle. Assessment isn't a one and done event; it's an ongoing process.

Unlike pulse surveys, which ask similar questions on a regular cadence, the culture survey is usually deployed one or two weeks after employee announcement day. Where pulse surveys are designed to help the acquirer learn how employees are feeling about the acquisition, the culture survey is designed to help the acquirer better understand the target company's ways of working. Culture surveys tend to be longer than pulse surveys and take most employees 15 to 20 minutes to complete.

Commercially Available Culture Surveys

There are several excellent commercially available M&A culture surveys on the market. These tools usually include dozens of questions and cover multiple dimensions of culture. They're validated and have been administered hundreds of times, allowing them to provide benchmark data. The firms offering these surveys typically offer extensive reporting, analysis, and culture integration support.

Do-it-yourself Culture Surveys

In some cases, the acquisition budget, timeline, or acquiring company's cultural norms don't allow the buyer to deploy a commercial survey, leaving the HR practitioner to choose between a do-it-yourself (DIY) approach or opting not to perform a culture survey.

Unless the HR practitioner has extensive training and experience with survey administration and interpretation, the DIY survey should be simple and follow the same design and participation principles used for pulse surveys (see Chapter 15).

Sample DIY Culture Survey Questions

This section provides several culture questions that HR practitioners can use if they create a DIY survey. The survey has the same look and feel as the pulse surveys to help employees complete the survey quickly and accurately. As always, the HR practitioner should apply professional judgment to the questions that will be asked of employees.

Please rate your level of agreement with each of the following statements related to the acquisition:

1	2	3	4	5	6	7
Strongly Disagree	Disagree	Somewhat Disagree	Neutral	Somewhat Agree	Agree	Strongly Agree

- Top leaders encourage and empower employees to make important decisions
- My work is guided by defined policies and processes
- Top leaders are open to new ideas and opinions about our work
- Our company does a good job of planning for the future and uses those plans to guide our decisions
- Most of our decisions are based on careful analysis
- Employees are encouraged to try new and innovative approaches, even if they might not work out
- I understand my role in the organization and do not expect it to change from day to day
- Our organization values broad knowledge over expertise
- The company provides frequent opportunities to learn about my coworkers outside of our day-to-day work
- We get the best results when we work independently or in smaller groups
- Top leaders effectively address employee issues and concerns
- It's easy for me to get the tools and resources I need to do my job
- It's okay if I miss my goals as long as I follow our processes

- Employees here are rewarded more for their individual performance than any other factor
- I often find myself working more quickly that I'd like
- If I'm able to complete my primary work quickly, it's okay if I leave early or take on special projects
- Changes to our organization and processes usually go well
- How we do things is rooted in tradition and we don't change them very often
- Top leaders share important decisions and how they were made
- I learn most of what I need to know through formal meetings and emails
- Communication from top leaders is both timely and frequent
- Top leaders do whatever it takes for our customers to view the company in a positive light
- I feel comfortable sharing the problems and challenges I face at work with my leaders
- Top leaders apply different standards to some employees
- I am proud of what our company does and what we stand for
- I am okay giving up personal time so the company can succeed
- The most important part of my job is coming up with good ideas
- My manager provides the coaching and mentoring I need
- My coworkers respect my time
- Top leaders treat employees fairly, regardless of level, role, work group, or personal characteristics like race, gender, sexual orientation, gender identity, disability, or other factors

Please provide your feedback on the following questions:
- What three words or phrases best describe [company name]'s culture?
- How would you describe [company name]'s management style?
- How do your leaders define success?

After the Survey

Culture surveys are different than pulse surveys, in that they're not attempting to directly measure the success of re-recruitment and culture change efforts that occur during the integration phase. This means the response to the culture survey will have a different look and feel from other employee listening activities.

After the culture survey closes, the HR practitioner should review the answers, comparing them to the cultural factors experienced by buy-side employees, which may require a separate buy-side survey administration. They can then prepare a report to share with both integration and leadership team members. The report should include the raw survey data, including both the net numeric scores of the scaled items and the complete text of any open-ended questions. Next, the report should include analysis of the results and how they change the earlier findings plotted on the risk assessment matrix (see Chapter 8). Once the risk assessment matrix is updated, the entire integration team should evaluate and update the communications plans and re-recruitment messages created in Chapter 13.

Finally, employees expect to hear back about the survey from the team. Since the survey isn't designed to drive action, the response is usually a high-level summary of the survey results. This can be as simple as sharing what employees said they like about the culture and what they think can be improved, alongside how this information will affect the integration plan.

Like all employee listening, failing to let employees know you heard their concerns can create challenges to employee morale. Only do a survey if you're going to let employees know you listened!

Chapter 17: Focus Groups

While surveys are useful for quickly and inexpensively gathering data from large groups of people, they lack the intimacy and interaction that's often required to truly understand what acquired employees are experiencing. This is where focus groups come into play.

A focus group is a moderated discussion that can help HR practitioners better understand what employees are thinking and how they're feeling about the acquisition, including how they're dealing with uncertainty-related stress, identity crisis, and cultural differences. Focus groups can also provide important information for re-recruitment efforts and updates to the communication plan.

Focus groups are most effective after the first one or two pulse surveys are completed and the culture survey responses are compiled, as they allow the HR practitioner to get deeper insight into the survey findings. However, they can be useful standalone exercises if the organization chooses not to survey target company employees.

Determine Who Participates

To encourage honest participation, most focus group sessions are kept small, with eight to twelve people participating. This means the HR practitioner will probably need to schedule multiple focus group sessions to ensure they're getting different viewpoints. If resources permit, it can be helpful to ensure each employee is invited to participate in one of the focus group sessions, even if they decline. Participation should always be voluntary and confidential.

The participants can be selected several ways, including members chosen at random or because of a common characteristic. Some HR practitioners look for a representative cross-section of the organization, others prefer to meet with groups made up of members of a specific department or location, high-potential employees, change champions (see Part 7), or line managers.

One Roundtable member recommends holding a focus group made up of people who actively resist the acquisition, allowing them to vent with one another rather than affecting employees who don't harbor such strong negative feelings. Another uses sign-up sheets and allows employees to self-select on a first-come, first-served basis. To ensure employees can openly and honestly share their opinions, it's often best to avoid creating groups where employees sit with members of the management team, as that can stifle conversation.

Create Meaningful Questions

The focus group should last no more than an hour, so the questions must be clear and relevant. Before finalizing the questions, step into your audience's shoes and ask 1) is the question easy to understand?, 2) do employees care about this question?, and 3) will we be able to take action on the responses?. If the answer to any of the questions is "no," consider rewriting or replacing the question with one that's a better fit for the audience. For best results, questions should be consistent between sessions.

To make this chapter an immediately useful focus group guide, a set of sample questions appears in the section covering how to conduct the focus group.

Finalize Focus Group Logistics

Once the participants have been selected and questions created, the integration team will need to decide who will moderate the session. The HR practitioner or integration leader are usually the best option, unless somebody in the focus group will be one of their direct reports. Focus groups generally last about one hour and can occur in person or virtually, depending on the circumstances.

Employee invitations should be sent at least a few days in advance and clearly state the meeting topic. In addition to meeting logistics like time, place, and purpose, the invitation should also include the questions that will be asked during the focus group. This gives employees time to think about their answers and come prepared for the discussion.

Conduct the Focus Group

One of the moderator's primary responsibilities is ensuring every employee in the room participates in the discussion. This requires a moderator who is both firm and personable. It can also be helpful to have a note taker, who can be another member of the integration team.

Both the moderator and note taker should remain neutral during the conversation, avoiding noticeably strong reactions to employee statements and opinions. Unless a statement is clearly false and requires immediate correction, the moderator should simply respond by acknowledging that they've heard the person's thoughts and concerns. Confrontation and correction should only be used in extreme circumstances.

In addition to employees' words, the moderator and note taker should watch employees' body language carefully. Employees who are reluctant to verbalize might share volumes with their body language. Realize, however, that body language is subjective making it important to clarify observations when possible.

A skilled moderator will work to ensure different viewpoints are welcome and heard. Statements like "Thanks for sharing that perspective, ____. What does the rest of the group think about that?" can invite discussion in a respectful way.

The moderator should ensure the group remains focused, allowing only tangents that contribute to the goals of the focus group. Finally, the moderator should ensure employees feel heard, which can be done by asking probing questions and paraphrasing responses.

Start with Introductions

The moderator should start by introducing themselves, their role, and the purpose of the meeting. They should open with a statement that establishes clear boundaries about the discussion, including the need to stay on topic, ensure everybody is sharing, and how employee responses will be captured.

This opening statement might sound something like:

"Hi, my name is Carol and I'm part of the HR team at XYZ Co. I've been in HR for about 10 years and have also been acquired once in my career and found myself feeling both nervous and excited going through that experience.

We're here today so I can hear your thoughts and opinions about how our two teams are coming together. Everyone received the questions in advance, and I'm interested in hearing what you have to say about them. We have a large group here today and I want to hear from each of you, so I might need to ask some of you to give shorter answers and encourage others of you to share what's on your mind.

Because I want to remember what you're telling me... *(if virtual)* I'm going to record the meeting. Or *(if in-person)* ...I've asked my colleague Jane to take notes. Of course, everything you say will be confidential. I will be sharing themes with our leaders, but I won't be going into detail about who said what. Let's get started."

The moderator can then go around the room, asking each employee to share their name, department, tenure, and anything else that's relevant to the conversation.

Warm-up with Icebreakers

Employees are often reluctant to jump right into focus group questions, so a warm-up exercise can be helpful for driving engagement.

Virtual icebreakers might include sharing words or phrases about how the integration is going, the acquired company's culture, or the attendee's feelings about a recent milestone. These can be put into word clouds, polls, or the chat feature.

In person icebreakers can include straightforward exercises where they finish the moderator's sentence or answer a question. For example, "One thing I like about becoming part of XYZ Co is ____." Or "If I could change one thing about this deal, it would be ____." In a low trust environment, employees can write their answers on a slip of paper that the facilitator will share with the group and invite comments on.

Ask Structured Questions

Once employees are engaged in the conversation, the moderator can begin asking the focus group questions. Because the sessions are only an hour long and everybody should have the chance to participate, most focus group sessions will only be able to cover three or four questions.

Remember, the questions should be clear, relevant, and consistent between sessions. A few sample questions are included below, but the moderator should exercise professional judgment when choosing which questions to include in the session. This includes questions that arise from analysis of the pulse and culture survey results. Some hypothetical examples are included in this list.

- What words or feelings come to mind when you think about your company's culture?
- How do you describe the integration to other people?
- What are your biggest hopes and fears about this integration process?
- What kinds of things would make you want to stay with the company after the integration is complete?
- How would you prefer to receive communications from the integration team?
- What's one thing we could do that would make your time at work more pleasant and productive?
- In the culture survey, about half of you described your founder as a visionary. Tell me more about that.
- In the last pulse survey, 36 percent of you had strong negative feelings about the acquisition. What do you think is behind that?

Close the Focus Group

As the focus group naturally winds down, or when there are only ten minutes left in the session, the moderator should let participants know the time is limited and they'll only be able to get opinions from a few other people. This is a great opportunity to acknowledge participants who have been silent and encourage them to share their thoughts. It's also an opportunity to ask a final catch-all question, like "What else would you like to share about what we've covered today?"

Once each attendee has been given the chance to share, the moderator can paraphrase the themes that have emerged during the discussion, ensuring they have accurately captured the prevailing mood of the group. The moderator can then close by thanking each participant for their time and let them know how the information gathered will be shared with leaders and what kind of follow up they can expect.

After the Focus Group

Once all the focus group sessions are complete, the moderator should evaluate the themes that emerged during the discussions and provide a final report to the integration team and business sponsors. This information should be evaluated alongside other cultural intelligence and employee listening findings.

The survey results should be used to adjust the culture risk assessment matrix (Chapter 8). Once the risk assessment matrix is updated, the entire integration team should evaluate and update the communications plan (Chapter 13).

When there are common themes, the integration team should communicate with the broader employee base. A simple communication might include "you said X, and we're doing Y." This lets employees know they've been heard and helps drive retention.

When there are individual concerns, the integration team should evaluate what changes can be made and what changes can't. The moderator should return to each employee who is owed follow up with a plan of action, clearly sharing what can and can't be changed, and a timeline for making changes to the situation when appropriate.

Like all employee listening, the focus group can be an effective way to understand what's going on with the employees. However, employee engagement can plummet if the integration team doesn't act on the information they've collected. If you aren't committed to listening to the employees and taking action, don't do the focus groups!

Chapter 18: Stay Interviews

When it comes to re-recruiting, long-term retention, and engagement of key employees, non-financial factors can be just as important as financial incentives. Figuring out which non-financial incentives will matter to an individual requires a good understanding of what motivates that employee, including their personal circumstances and aspirations as well as their career goals and workplace needs.

Common employee motivators include professional growth and development, relevant leadership opportunities, and meaningful recognition for a job well done. Other engagement factors will be idiosyncratic and uncovering them requires a one-on-one conversation with the employee. Examples of distinctive individual motivators include span of control, job titles, or personal commitment to their colleagues.

This chapter discusses how to use stay interviews to uncover which non-financial factors will motivate a key employee to not only stay with the organization but will also generate increased engagement and productivity.

According to the Society for Human Resource Management[1], companies that have successfully used stay interviews see decreased turnover and increased first year retention, saving hundreds of thousands of dollars in replacement costs and increasing productivity and profitability.

Stay interviews are different from exit interviews, which occur after an employee has resigned. Asking for feedback after somebody quits is like asking for marriage counseling after the divorce has been filed. The information can be helpful for your next relationship but isn't likely to improve the current situation.

The stay interview, on the other hand, allows the integration team to get in front of potential problems, thereby making key employees more likely to stay. While only 25 percent of employers currently use stay interviews to retain their key people[2], more and more firms are adopting them every year because they tend to be more effective and useful than exit interviews.

Decide Who Gets Interviewed

As the integration team designed the future organization (Chapter 11), they identified which roles and individuals are critical to realizing deal value. The employees in these roles should be first in line to complete a stay interview. Even if the organization design isn't finalized, it's prudent to meet with employees who are obviously crucial to organizational success.

In some cases, the team will find it necessary to interview every employee. This is most appropriate for service organizations where the people are the product. Interviewing the entire team might also happen in situations where most of the team is selected for a stay interview, and it would be culturally insensitive to exclude a few team members from these discussions. Remember employees talk to one another and there is no such thing as a secret conversation when people are trying to make sense of their world.

Finalize Interview Logistics

Once the integration team has determined who they want to interview, they will need to decide who conducts the interviews. In most cases, the employee's direct manager is the best person to facilitate these discussions. However, it might be more appropriate for the person's skip level manager or a key company leader to host the interview in some cases. If these leaders aren't able to conduct the interview, the sell-side HR team (if there is one), the buy-side HR leader, or integration team can step in.

It's critical to remember that employees are understandably skittish after an acquisition announcement and getting an unexpected meeting notice labeled "Stay Interview," "Career Discussion," or "HR Meeting" could do more harm than good. Instead, let the employee know beforehand that they are important to the organization, and you want to find out what they're thinking and how they're feeling about the acquisition and their place in the new organization. It's helpful to send the questions in advance so the employee will have time to think about their responses.

Stay interviews generally last between 30 and 60 minutes. Be sure this time is dedicated to the stay interview and not mixed with other matters. Setting aside this time allows both the employee and interviewer to focus on what's going on with the employee and communicates to the employee how critical they are to the organization.

Conduct the Interview

Unless the target company culture is highly formal, a casual and conversational tone is usually best for the stay interview. The interviewer should open the meeting by restating the goals of the interview. Employees should know that the interviewer is taking notes for future reflection and some parts of the conversation might be shared with members of the integration team so they can consider any questions or concerns the employee has.

The employee should understand the interviewer won't be able to take immediate action, and the interviewer should avoid making any promises during the conversation. While it might be tempting to respond to the employee's points, the interviewer needs to spend much more time listening than talking. Interviewers must resist the urge to spend time during the interview on fixing problems or correcting misperceptions and truly listen to the employee. The better approach is for the interviewer to take the feedback away and arrange a follow-on meeting, especially if they're unclear about the path forward or don't have the answers to a specific question.

Sample Stay Interview Questions

The stay interview is designed to help the leadership team understand how key employees are reacting to the acquisition. The interviewer should walk away with a better understanding of what the employee is thinking and how they're feeling (reaction questions). They should also leave understanding what factors make the employee want to stay (retention questions) and why they might want to leave (attrition questions).

The questions are all open-ended and include a mix of reaction, retention, and attrition factors, allowing the manager a holistic view of the employee's experience. Interviewers might want to reorder, update, or replace some questions, but they should be sure to cover all three factors.

Reaction questions

- How are you feeling about the acquisition?
- Where do you see yourself fitting into the future organization?
- What can we do to help make this a positive experience?
- What else would you like to say about the acquisition?

Retention questions

- What do you most look forward to when you come into work?
- Which assignments have you enjoyed the most?
- How can we support your work-life balance?
- What development opportunities would you like to have?

Attrition questions

- What do you like least about working here now?
- Which parts of your job do you most dread?
- Which of your skills and talents are we not making the most of?
- If you could change one thing about the acquisition, what would it be?

Conclude the Interview

When the interviewer has gone through all the questions, they should take a few moments to summarize what they heard, asking the employee for clarification where necessary. Again, the interviewer should avoid making commitments unless they're absolutely certain they can keep them.

Finally, the interviewer should sincerely thank the employee for their time and willingness to share. This is also a fantastic opportunity to authentically acknowledge the employee's specific contributions to the company and the team, ending the meeting by showing the employee they are truly valued and important to the organization.

After the Interview

Once the integration team has interviewed all of the key employees, they should convene to review the information they've gathered during the stay interviews. When there are common themes, the integration team should communicate what they've heard and how they intend to react back to the broader employee base, adjusting the re-recruitment key messages and broader communications plan (Chapter 13).

When there are individual concerns, the integration team should evaluate what changes can and can't be made to the employee's work experience. The initial interviewer should return to each employee with a plan of action, clearly sharing what can and can't be changed and a timeline for making changes to the situation when appropriate.

While the stay interview is a powerful tool for getting information about your team's needs, you can significantly damage team morale if you don't do anything with the information you've gathered. If you aren't committed to listening to the employees and taking action, don't do the interviews!

Part 7: The First 100 Days

Both culture change and M&A integration can take years to complete, depending on the magnitude of the change and complexity of the integration. Because business conditions change so quickly, most seasoned acquirers use a 100-day plan to kick off the integration and change period, a convention we follow in this book.

The 100-day period begins on employee announcement day (Chapter 14). Shortly following announcement—on day one or two—employees should receive the first pulse survey (Chapter 15). The remaining 98 days are a flurry of employee communications (Chapter 13), employee listening activities (Part 6), and the remaining critical cultural integration events covered in Part 7. A timeline showing how all of the elements fit together is included in Chapter 22.

Unlike traditional hires, acquired employees are juggling their integration duties with their other job responsibilities, making it critical to have a strategy for the first 100 days. Employees are subject to an avalanche of communications and required activities, leaving them buried in actions and priorities. Somebody on the integration team should be responsible for coordinating all employee communications during this period of re-recruitment. Leading acquirers also find it helpful to involve line managers and enlist change champions during this critical early period.

Involve Line Managers

Line managers are an employee's most trusted source of information[1]. In addition to the strategic visibility that comes from better access to company leaders, especially in organizations with fewer than 100 people, line managers are responsible for translating strategy into the day-to-day work of the employee. Furthermore, the line manager and employee usually have regular contact with one another, engendering trust as they've worked together.

Unfortunately, most line managers haven't received adequate development[2], leaving them challenged to operate effectively in the best of times. Overcoming this skill gap during M&A means the integration team needs to be proscriptive, providing advance notice, training, and talking points to line managers. Leading practices include hosting special training sessions and allowing line managers to preview documents like FAQs, offer letters, and other communications.

Enlist Change Champions

In addition to managers and others with formal authority, most organizations have a handful of influential employees who can be enlisted as change champions. These employees are often easily identified by sell-side leadership or can be found using organizational network analysis or other tools if they aren't apparent.

Change champions are people who are excited about the acquisition and can accelerate cultural integration by acting as a bridge between the integration team and other employees. Change champions often hear issues and concerns that formal leaders do not. They can also help counter rumors and disinformation with facts about the deal. Like managers, change champions benefit from special training sessions geared toward their roles.

Cultural Integration Requires Time and Money

As you read this book, it became clear that culture clash is the default setting and overcoming culture clash requires intention, time, and effort. The work of cultural integration can't be delegated to HR or the integration leader. Successful cultural integration demands the business sponsor's time, attention, and budget.

Unlike mechanical parts—which don't argue when they're repositioned, upgraded, or replaced—people resist imposed change. Leadership is required to overcome this resistance and drive the deal thesis.

I've heard some top executives say, "all of this change management is just a distraction." To those leaders I reply, "your team is distracted the minute employees learn about the acquisition." When a business leader fails to do the work required for cultural integration, that leader is choosing to destroy the value of their M&A investment.

Additionally, many business leaders don't adequately fund integration activities. They'll spend millions of dollars on the transaction itself and then skimp when it comes to cultural integration. That's like buying a luxury vehicle and then refusing to put fuel in the tank. Congratulations, you now have a nice car that isn't going anywhere.

Right-sizing Integration Efforts

As we noted in the introduction, the tools and techniques in this book are optimized for the typical transaction, a larger acquirer purchasing a company with fewer than 100 employees. While most of these techniques can be scaled to larger transactions, there are likely to be significant differences.

The 100-employee threshold is important to understand because our brains appear to be wired for social groups of around 150 people, most of whom are work contacts in our current society. In 1992, Dr. Robin Dunbar, an anthropologist and primate researcher, hypothesized that the human neocortex is only capable of supporting around 150 stable social relationships[3]. These relationships include family, friends, social contacts, and co-workers. This phenomenon is commonly referred to as Dunbar's Number.

Dunbar's Number has been subject to intense scrutiny, but the concept appears to be valid, even if the number of relationships vary based on setting and individual characteristics. A deeper discussion of Dunbar's Number is out of scope for this guide, but the application of this concept to cultural integration is intuitive. It's harder for company leaders to have strong relationships with 500 people than it is for them to have strong relationships with 100 people. Keep this reality in mind when scaling these integration techniques for transactions with more than 100 employees.

Chapter 19: Managing Employee Transitions

There are several different psychological, organizational, and legal transitions employees might experience as part of a merger or acquisition. These transitions include voluntary and involuntary exits as well as job changes and transfers between employing legal entities. In many cases, employees will remain in their positions without any changes to the job or employer of record, experiencing only a psychological transition.

The magnitude of the employee transition will depend a great deal on the integration model. If the organization remains standalone, there might not be any changes and the suggestions here might not apply at all. Likewise, business transformations might require additional communication steps, as they tend to be more disruptive than the partial integrations and full assimilations that are the model for this chapter.

No matter what type of integration is planned, the acquiring organization's ability to support employees through their transitions is essential to driving deal value. These steps are critical to overcoming culture clash because they support re-recruitment, provide certainty, and invite adoption of a new identity.

Employee transitions are subject to intense regulation in most of the world, unlike most U.S.-based employees who work at will. HR practitioners are encouraged to work with labor attorneys who understand the M&A provisions of relevant employment law in any country where they're doing deals when creating the 100-day plan.

Exiting Employees

Employees exit for a number of reasons, including redundancies, failure to meet minimum requirements, poor behavior, or by choice. In smaller organizations, any employee exiting will be noticed and create ripples in the organization. Cultural integration will be delayed if there are concerns about waves of employee exits, and organizations are encouraged to handle involuntary exits in a timely fashion. The buyer must also ensure the process for determining who exits involuntarily is fair and compliant with local law.

The most common reason employees are involuntarily exited is redundancy, with approximately 30 percent of employees made redundant in same-industry mergers[1]. In these cases, the deal model calls for employee exits to meet financial targets. Layoffs should be carefully considered, as the cost savings that come from terminating employees are sometimes overshadowed by the increased costs of employee replacement and retraining. Productivity can also take a significant hit due to lowered morale and resentment against the acquirer.

In some deals, employees are asked to compete for their positions, going through a new selection process to keep the jobs they currently hold. This process is suboptimal and will almost always result in increased attrition and lower morale, which will in turn destroy deal value. To avoid unnecessarily alienating employees, thereby stalling cultural integration, the selection process must feel necessary, fair and be clearly communicated. The process should also be administered quickly, to avoid prolonging feelings of uncertainty.

Redundancy layoffs that occur as the result of M&A are strictly regulated in many countries and might be prohibited. One of the reasons it's important to have HR involved in due diligence and synergy planning is to help the deal team understand if the people-related synergies that are included in the financial model are going to be an option under local law. The HR practitioner should consult with a local expert before making any redundancy plans.

Employees might also be involuntarily exited if they don't pass required background checks and drug screens or are otherwise not qualified to work at the acquiring organization. These layoffs should be considered similarly to redundancy exits.

Involuntary exits affect the entire organization and should be considered carefully. Firing a group of acquired employees becomes a focal point for the default culture clash and will exacerbate the *us against them* feelings that exist in the acquired organization.

Exits can occur before or after the deal closes, which means responsibility for the process might belong to either the buy- or sell-side HR team. Before redundancies are announced, the deal team must understand who will be responsible for managing the layoff process and which severance rules will govern. This might be stipulated in the definitive agreement, collective bargaining agreement, or local law.

Once these decisions are made, the integration team will need to create a layoff timeline and communications plan separate from the rest of the communications workstream. Larger-scale exit planning can be challenging, and consultation with an expert is often helpful.

Sometimes employees don't want to be part of the newly combined company and will choose to exit. The deal team will need to decide how to handle severances, if offered, to those who voluntarily exit. Organizations don't usually offer severance to employees who leave voluntarily.

Employees might also be terminated for cause if they're unable to appropriately manage their reactions to the acquisition. These types of exits are a challenge in the best of times and are exceptionally difficult during the integration period. In addition to consulting with an expert, the management team will need to ensure messaging is appropriate to the circumstances.

No matter the reasons employees exit, the acquirer is best served if they're handled respectfully and follow a well-designed process. The remaining employees will watch the process very closely and judge the acquirer based on how well the exits are managed.

Remaining Employees

Since culture is *how people get things done in the workplace,* the employees who remain with the organization will either help or hinder cultural integration. Even when there are no involuntary exits, all remaining employees must be re-recruited, quickly overcoming their uncertainty and rapidly developing a shared identity with buy-side employees. The integration team must effectively lead the remaining employees through their transitions and onboarding (Chapter 20) to preserve deal value.

The remainder of this chapter is dedicated to managing the variety of basic work transitions experienced by the remaining employees. These include changes to total rewards, job title and responsibilities, management structure, legal employer, and location. Planning for these changes must occur before they are communicated to employees

(Chapter 11) and will affect the timing of this activity. In general, the sooner this information is communicated to employees, the better the results will be.

For simplicity, we will refer to this as the employee offer process, though the details and mechanisms will change from deal to deal. Even when employees don't experience any changes to their work situation, the acquisition will require a psychological transition from one team to the other. In those circumstances, communications mirroring the offer process can accelerate cultural integration.

The best person to support employees through this transition process is typically the line manager or a member of the sell-side leadership team. To successfully hold these conversations, the leader or manager must be trained on the offer process, receive a preview of the changes that will occur, and have access to resources that will support them as messengers. Furthermore, each of these changes should be incorporated in the communication plan (Chapter 13).

Host an Employee Offer Town Hall

Shortly before employees learn how any changes to their work will affect them personally, the HR practitioner should organize another town hall. The employee offer town hall should be designed to continue the re-recruitment process, providing additional certainty and getting employees excited about their new workplace identity. The elements of a successful employee offer town hall are detailed below.

Open the meeting

While HR will own most of the meeting content, it's exceptionally helpful to have sell-side leaders start the meeting, explain why the team has been called together, and lend their support to the buy-side leaders and the HR practitioner. Opening the meeting is also an opportunity for the leader to reflect on the integration so far, using the time to acknowledge the team's effort and successes despite the stress of the transaction.

For this opening to be effective, the sell-side leader should be involved in the integration planning activities and understand significant changes to the employee experience. In addition to gaining the sell-side leader's alignment on the plan, the sell-side leader can then help shape the way messages are delivered, ensuring they will aid cultural integration.

Once the sell-side leader has opened the meeting, one of the buy-side leaders, usually the business sponsor or integration leader, should announce any general updates they would like to share. This might include important organizational decisions, like structure or leadership changes.

Next, the business sponsor can generate excitement by sharing updates on the buyer's business, highlighting how the remaining employees will be critical to the combined company's success. This is also a strong opportunity to share alignment between the buyer's mission, vision, and values, and those of the acquired company and team. The more effectively the business sponsor can build these bridges, the more effective the cultural integration efforts will be.

Finally, the business sponsor should express their excitement for the integration and reiterate the value the acquired team brings to the firm. They can also share any victories the combined team has already experienced. The business sponsor then turns the meeting over to HR.

Share the employee value proposition

At its core, the employee offer town hall is an opportunity to re-recruit the acquired employees. The HR practitioner should continue thanking employees for the integration work they've done so far and share their excitement about the employees joining the buyer's team.

The employee offer town hall can be more effective if the buyer has appropriate recruitment videos or slide decks that share why the employer is a great place to work. Coordination with the buy-side talent acquisition team can be very helpful.

Explain changes to total rewards

The next part of the meeting is perhaps one of the most challenging change leadership opportunities that arises during a deal. This is because even when employees feel secure in the knowledge that they have a job, the third of our big three questions is unanswered. Employees remain nervous about whether their job will be as good.

Even when changes to pay, benefits, and perks are overall more favorable, employees will be sensitive to benefits and perks that they feel are being taken away. They're usually less focused on benefits and perks that are added to their total rewards.

Changes should be communicated as quickly and empathetically as possible if employees are expected to support cultural integration. The HR practitioner should share how decisions that change total rewards were made, including enough detail for employees to understand how the changes affect their unique circumstances.

Communicate other HR changes

After communicating changes to total rewards, the HR practitioner should share details of any other changes to the employees' work situation. These announcements often include changes to the legal employer (i.e., moving onto the buyer's payroll) or other employment processes that will affect the employees.

This section is usually not appropriate for announcing major organizational changes or milestones. Those should be shared by a leader at the start of the meeting.

Share details of the offer process

The next part of the town hall should focus on how the offer process will be managed. It should include how and when employees will receive communications about their future employment and how their manager will be involved in the process. Employees should also understand if the offers are negotiable and the date by when countersigned offers should be returned to HR, if applicable.

Manage employee Q&A

The last part of the town hall should be an employee Q&A session where employees ask questions of both the sell-side leaders, business sponsor, and HR practitioner. Just like the announcement day town hall, it can be helpful for a few sell-side leaders to come with prepared questions. This will ensure the most frequent questions are answered and give employees social permission to ask their own questions.

Communicate Employee Offers

The most common way to formally notify U.S.-based employees of changes to their work is via an offer or transfer letter, even if written notice isn't legally required based on the transaction details. In other parts of the world, there are different requirements. Consultation with an employment attorney familiar with M&A transactions in the affected locations is highly recommended to ensure compliance and cultural sensitivity. For simplicity, we will refer to these as offer letters, regardless of how they're communicated and delivered.

Offer letters typically contain several key elements, including employing entity, job title, manager, location, start date, and total rewards. If the employee's job description changes, consider including it with the offer. If there are any contingencies—such as background checks, drug screens, or the deal closing—that must occur before the offer becomes effective, mention those as well.

Some employees will be given special retention packages as part of their offer, and those packages should be communicated at the same time as the rest of the offer. Similarly, if the employee's offer is temporary in nature, include the anticipated end date and any retention or severance provisions.

Regardless of whether these changes are communicated in writing, employees deserve the dignity of a conversation about their offer. This means either the line manager or a more senior buy-side leader should connect with each employee, explaining the details of their offer. The leader should also share how the employee will contribute to the company's future and express their support for the acquisition. Finally, the leader should reinforce the process and timeline for accepting the offer, including whether there is room for negotiation.

Offer Additional Support

Because the employee offer town hall is a re-recruitment event, the integration team should consider providing additional support to employees and managers. This support can include offering swag and hosting leader and HR office hours, like what's done on employee announcement day (Chapter 14). This is also an opportune time to

Klint C. Kendrick

update the FAQs with details on the offer process and changes to total rewards.

Chapter 20: Onboarding Acquired Employees

After the deal has closed, the remaining employees are likely to experience some changes to their work experience, including possible changes to total rewards and the employer of record. The onboarding process guides employees through these changes, and when done properly accelerates the cultural integration process.

As we discussed in the prior chapter, changes to the work setting are less likely to happen when the target remains standalone. Similarly, a business transformation can involve more change and require additional support. The suggestions in this chapter are optimized for a partial integration or full assimilation.

The onboarding process requires quite a bit of backend preparation, including ensuring smooth transitions to new HRIS, payroll, and benefits systems. One of the worst things that can happen during integration is an employee not getting an accurate and timely paycheck. Thoroughly pre-planning the onboarding process makes this error much less likely to happen.

Orientation Town Hall

The onboarding process kicks off with an orientation town hall. If the employees are changing legal entities (i.e., moving from the seller's payroll to the buyer's payroll), orientation should coincide with the payroll transfer. If employees are remaining with the seller's legal entity, then the orientation town hall schedule is not as critical, and the agenda should be updated to reflect deal particulars.

The overall theme of employee orientation is one of welcome. Like other town halls, the sell-side leadership team and business sponsor should be on hand to welcome employees and share their excitement for the transaction. The meeting can then be handed off to HR.

The day's agenda can be based on the acquirer's new employee orientation program but must be modified to reflect the way acquired employees are joining the organization. The acquired employees are joining as a group and are already busy with their day-to-day responsibilities. This means their orientation should be practical, sharing the most important processes they will be expected to follow on the job. These typically include HR and IT but might also include procurement and other back-office functions depending on the deal.

New Hire Paperwork

Unlike a traditionally hired employee, acquired employees might already have much of the required paperwork on file. Nevertheless, employees might need to complete many of the same forms as a traditional hire, depending on the nature of the transaction. When in doubt, contact an employment attorney who understands M&A.

If employees are moving to a new HR system, it can be useful to request updates to their personal information, including home address and emergency contacts. If employees are changing payroll providers or benefits plans, they might need to complete additional paperwork to ensure these important items are handled correctly.

Employees might also need to complete new tax paperwork and immigration forms to satisfy government requirements. In some cases, the employees should be asked to provide demographic information to ensure compliance with applicable employment regulations.

Finally, the employees might become subject to new handbooks, policies, and procedures as part of their employment. This can include codes of conduct, intellectual property assignments, confidentiality agreements, safety rules, and other important policies. In some cases, employees will be asked to sign these documents and commit to following the policies they reference.

Welcome Celebration

Orientation day is a pivotal event for many employees. It represents the official end of one identity and the official start of another. While employees might still cling to their old identity for some time, a celebration can start cementing the new identity in the employee's psyche.

The sell-side leadership team should be involved in planning the celebration event to be sure it strikes the right tone. Both buy- and sell-side leaders should be actively involved in the event. Employees will notice who is participating and who has stepped out. Remember, we are still re-recruiting acquired employees at this point. Just because they've accepted an employment offer doesn't mean they aren't job hunting.

Mandatory Training

Many organizations require mandatory training for all new employees, and acquired employees are often subject to those rules. Because these employees don't have the luxury of easing into jobs like traditional hires, the HR practitioner should work with business leaders to understand how to ensure acquired employees have the time and resources necessary to complete the training.

Some organizations bring employees together and complete the mandatory training as a group, a tactic that ensures everybody completes the training on time with minimal disruption. Others choose to leave training to the individual employee. Regular status updates to acquired company managers can help ensure training gets done on time.

Cultural Integration Activities

During cultural due diligence, the HR practitioner and deal team identified and assessed potential areas of culture clash based on the five key drivers and deal-specific considerations. These findings will be deal-specific and will require deal-specific mitigations. The onboarding period is often the ideal time to implement the mitigation plans that were created earlier in the deal.

One member of the HR M&A Roundtable shared a situation where the two sales teams were blended, and the acquired sales team members were expected to adjust their selling process to match the buyer's method. Despite each team member keeping their old commission program, the changes in the sales approach were psychologically significant and the sales team required a lot of additional training and support.

Having encountered this challenge before, their initial cultural integration plan included weekly meetings for the sales team, in addition to frequent one-on-one meetings with both buy- and sell-side leaders to ensure the sales team could successfully adjust.

Another Roundtable member worked on a deal where most of the acquired R&D employees were completely moved into one of the acquirer's smaller divisions. The deal thesis required the teams to work together closely, creating new and innovative products with their combined expertise. To accelerate cultural integration, the buy- and sell-side leaders created several project teams with equal representation from each side of the deal, and leadership responsibilities equally divided between the two organizations.

The HR practitioner should look at the overall onboarding plan and ensure that significant cultural diligence items are addressed in the first 100 days. These will be deal specific and might require creative thinking to accelerate integration and overcome culture clash.

Chapter 21: Buddy Programs

When employees onboard through traditional routes, they're surrounded by colleagues who have figured out how things get done in the workplace. In other words, they're surrounded by people who understand the culture.

As we've noted throughout this book, acquired employees don't have the same benefit. They join as a group, leaving them confused as a group. They're frequently separate from the acquirer's physical space, making watercooler conversations impossible. They're also expected to continue performing their day-to-day responsibilities, with little time dedicated to transitioning the small things that aren't covered in formal onboarding programs.

One of the most effective ways to close the gap between the acquired employee's isolated experience and the traditional hire's supported onboarding is a buddy program. Buddy programs pair people from the buy side with people from the sell side with the goal of helping new employees successfully acculturate.

Buddy programs are most useful in partial integration or full assimilation deals, where employees in most roles will benefit from a buddy. The program is less useful in a standalone acquisition, though certain leadership or back-office roles will benefit from having a reliable contact in the acquirer's organization. The programs are most difficult to implement in a business transformation since everybody is moving along the same change curve.

This chapter outlines some of the basic steps for running a successful buddy program.

Selecting Buddies

Buddy relationships are informal and designed to help employees adapt to the acquiring company's culture. Buddies offer advice to acquired employees, connect them with company resources, and help them navigate the acquirer's organization. Most buddies spend about an hour a week when the program starts, and the responsibility tapers down over the acquired employee's first several months on the job.

Unlike coaches, mentors, and managers, buddies aren't responsible for setting goals, managing performance, or developing professional skills. In many cases, the buddy won't know how to do the acquired employee's job, making it easier to focus on helping the employee navigate the new culture.

A successful buddy program relies on volunteers who want to assist with onboarding their new colleagues. Buddies should have strong communication skills and be positive about the company. They need to understand and be engaged in the acquirer's culture, meaning the buddy should have at least a year with the acquirer. Finally, buddy candidates should be good performers whose manager trusts them to work with new team members.

Buddies should expect to benefit from the program as they contribute to its success. Buddy program participants will grow their networks and develop key leadership skills, including the ability to motivate others and influence without direct authority. They will also be gaining a new perspective about their firm and could form a lasting friendship.

People who would be great buddies are usually busy with other organizational responsibilities, so it can be helpful to offer buddies something extra. A member of the HR M&A Roundtable had problems recruiting buddies until they found budget to give each buddy $50 a month for buddy activities, which is enough for lunch for two and a few cups of coffee. They haven't had problems finding qualified buddies since adding the incentive.

Matching Buddies with Acquired Employees

Once buddies are selected, the HR practitioner will need to match them with acquired employees. Some firms choose to make matches based on common characteristics, like location, alma mater, or demographic similarities. Others keep the assignments random.

While buddies can come from any department, it's helpful if buddies come from other groups in the company. This ensures the acquired employee is meeting people from across the organization. It also lowers the risk of a group's internal politics affecting the buddy relationship.

Some buddies can manage three or four relationships simultaneously, but this isn't optimal. Managing multiple buddies can quickly morph from a one-to-one relationship into a one-to-many situation that doesn't fulfill the objectives of the buddy program.

Managing the Buddy Program

Buddies are often nervous at the start of the program, making training important for ensuring program effectiveness. The training session is a great opportunity to set expectations, provide sample agendas, and let buddies know where to go when they need help. If a buddy program has been run before, or the acquirer already has a buddy program for new hires, a panel of experienced buddies is a great way to energize the buddies-to-be.

Once the buddies have been trained, the two buddies need to meet one another. Some HR practitioners introduce the buddies while others leave that responsibility to the buy-side buddy. No matter how introductions are managed, buddies should be connected within a day of the orientation town hall. This gives the acquired employee an additional support person right away and allows the HR practitioner to quickly manage new buddy assignments if necessary.

Once buddies have been introduced, they may need assistance getting the relationship started. The HR practitioner can facilitate this process by offering guidelines for the buddies, including suggestions for meeting frequency and topics. During the first month, buddies should meet at least weekly. For the next two months, the meetings will occur every other week. Finally, buddies will meet at least once a month for months four, five, and six.

The first meeting should be introductory, giving the buddies a chance to learn about one another. If buddies are face-to-face, a small budget to cover coffee or lunch will make the initial meeting more effective.

The second meeting can include a tour of the workplace, whether the workplace is virtual or in-person. A face-to-face tour can include interesting and useful locations, including which departments sit where, restroom locations, ATMs, and eateries. It can also include good people to know, including office support staff or people in IT. If the team is virtual, a tour of the company intranet site, overview of the organization chart, and ways to reach helpful people should be on the agenda.

The third and fourth meetings tend to be more open-ended, with the buddy catching up on items that weren't covered in the first two meetings, sharing general insights into the company's culture, and continuing to make introductions to key people in the organization.

Finally, the HR practitioner should measure the success of the program using a survey or other check-in mechanism. Any feedback the program participants offer can be used to enhance future buddy programs.

Part 8: Bringing it All Together

Now that you understand the basics of cultural assessment and integration, we can turn our attention to applying what you've learned. The first chapter in this section outlines the major cultural assessment and integration milestones that arise in a typical deal. The second chapter discusses ways to measure cultural integration success.

Chapter 22: A Sample Timeline

Once we understand the concepts introduced throughout this book, it's time to use them to form a cohesive plan. This chapter provides a basic order of operations for the key activities that occur during cultural assessment and integration. The timeline is aligned with the deal lifecycle, which is shown below.

Buying A House

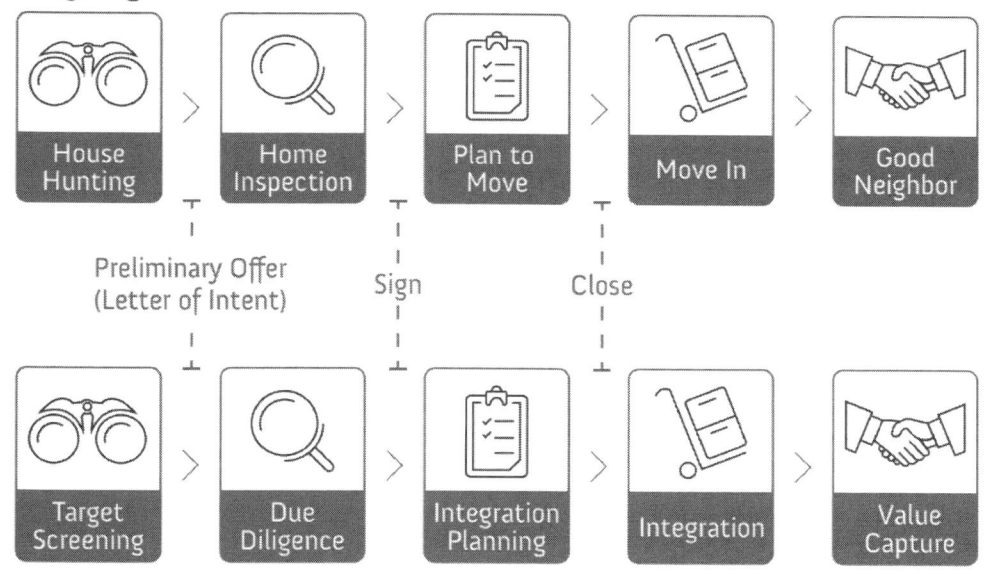

House Hunting > Home Inspection > Plan to Move > Move In > Good Neighbor

Preliminary Offer (Letter of Intent) — Sign — Close

Target Screening > Due Diligence > Integration Planning > Integration > Value Capture

Buying A Company

Creating the sample timeline required several assumptions around the transaction timeline and access to sell-side leaders. These assumptions are included in the text along with other tips. Like everything we've discussed in this book, you will need to adapt this plan to fit the circumstances of your M&A deal.

Cultural Due Diligence

Cultural due diligence includes all activities required to identify the potential sources of culture clash on your deal, including the five key drivers (Chapter 4) and deal-specific considerations (Chapter 5). It's made up of the target screening and formal due diligence phases of the deal.

Target Screening

Target screening begins when the HR professional is informed about the deal and continues until the letter of intent is signed. This timeline assumes HR is engaged during target screening. If HR isn't engaged, the three target screening items included below will need to be reviewed during formal due diligence.

- Begin cultural due diligence (Chapter 6)
    - Investigate public information
    - Hear expert opinions
    - Review the confidential information memorandum

- Provide the target screening brief (Chapter 9)

Chapter 22: A Sample Timeline

Formal Due Diligence

The formal due diligence period begins when the LOI is signed and ends when the deal is signed. This timeline assumes HR has been engaged since target screening, which isn't often the case. If HR wasn't involved in target screening, they will need to review public information, expert opinions, and the confidential information memorandum during formal due diligence.

The last step listed in this phase is early integration planning, which might be necessary to complete before the transaction is signed. Early integration planning requires coordination between the business sponsor, integration team, and key sell-side leaders before the deal is announced. If any of these parties are unavailable, early planning activities should be pushed to after the deal is announced.

- Finalize cultural due diligence (Chapter 7)
    - Review target screening findings (Chapter 6)
    - Examine seller-provided documents
    - Conduct due diligence interviews
    - Complete site visits
    - Hold the post-diligence huddle

- Provide the due diligence report (Chapter 9)

- Create the communications plan (Chapter 13)

- Support early integration planning (Chapter 11)
    - Leadership calibration
    - Organization design
    - Total rewards alignment

- Deal signed

193

Cultural Integration

Cultural integration begins when employees learn about the deal and might continue for prolonged periods. This timeline includes the employee announcement day, first 100 days, and longer-term integration items.

While our deal lifecycle illustration shows integration planning, integration, and value capture running in sequence, they often overlap during the speed of an M&A integration. Agility is key when working on M&A deals.

Employee Announcement Day

Employee announcement day usually occurs shortly after the deal is signed, as many firms are obligated to let the public or government know about a deal once it's signed. If these obligations don't exist, the integration team might want to delay employee announcement day until more planning has been done. Delaying the announcement must be balanced with ensuring employees have time to process any changes being made to their individual employment situation before those changes become effective.

- Facilitate employee announcement day events (Chapter 14)
    - Conduct a manager meeting
    - Hold an employee town hall
    - Offer corporate swag
    - Host an announcement day celebration
    - Staff leader and HR office hours

- Distribute FAQs to managers and employees (Chapter 13)

- Launch first employee pulse survey (Chapter 15)

Chapter 22: A Sample Timeline

Integration Planning (Days 2 to 30)

The integration planning portion of the timeline begins after employee announcement day and ends when the transaction closes. The timeline assumes this process will only take 30 days, but this phase might be skipped altogether—in the case of simultaneous sign and close transactions—or go for years while regulatory approvals are obtained.

If there is simultaneous sign and announce, or there is a short period between the deal being signed and closed, integration planning should be done in parallel with due diligence. If the period between sign and close exceeds 30 days, ensure regular employee communications, and continue employee listening to assist cultural integration.

Finally, this phase assumes an employee offer event is necessary to align with the deal structure, local regulations, or cultural expectations. Extending offers also requires a finalized organizational and total rewards alignment plan, which might not be possible until after close.

- Complete integration planning (Chapter 11)
    - Leadership calibration
    - Organization design
    - Total rewards alignment

- Share results of first pulse survey (Chapter 15)

- Train managers on the offer process and provide previews of employee offers (Chapter 19)

- Host employee offer town hall (Chapter 19). If offers are not part of the plan, host a general town hall for employees

- Communicate employee offers (Chapter 19)

- Send second pulse survey after offer town hall and share results when appropriate (Chapter 15)

- Deal closes

195

Integration (Days 31 to 60)

The first integration period in our timeline begins when the transaction closes and ends when employees are transferred to the buyer's payroll. The timeline assumes that employees will transfer payrolls as part of the deal and that this process will only take 30 days.

If employees won't be required to transfer employers, this integration period will end once employees are asked to accept new terms and conditions, like updated handbooks, policies, and procedures.

In the event the employee transfer process is expected to take longer than 30 days, build in a regular cadence of employee communications and continue to use employee listening techniques to maximize engagement and minimize attrition.

Finally, if employee offers weren't extended during integration planning, they may need to be extended during this part of the integration.

- Acknowledge that the deal has closed

- Distribute updated manager and employee FAQs (Chapter 13)

- Send culture survey (Chapter 16)

- Convene employee focus groups (Chapter 17)

- Share results of culture survey and focus groups (Chapters 16 and 17)

- Hold third employee town hall. Communicate employee offers if this was not done before the deal closed (Chapter 19)

- Send third pulse survey after employee town hall (Chapter 15)

- Share results of third pulse survey

- Finalize employee transfer

Chapter 22: A Sample Timeline

Integration (Days 61 to 100)

The second integration period in our timeline begins when employees are transferred to the buyer's payroll and ends when the employee onboarding process is complete. If employees won't be required to transfer employers, this integration period begins once employees are asked to accept new terms and conditions, like updated handbooks, policies, and procedures.

This timeline assumes that the process will take about 40 days and is designed to coincide with the typical 100-day plan used in M&A planning.

- Acknowledge that employees have transferred

- Distribute updated manager and employee FAQs (Chapter 13)

- Begin formal onboarding process with orientation town hall (Chapter 20)

- Send fourth pulse survey after town hall and share results when appropriate (Chapter 15)

- Launch buddy program (Chapter 21)

- Manage any outstanding changes planned for the first 100 days, such as location moves, redundant employee exits, etc.

- Continue training employees on important changes to how things get done at work

- Host final town hall where the longer-term plan is shared

Value Capture (Days 101+)

The first 100 days are a whirlwind of activity, with employees experiencing some of the most rapid and significant changes in their careers. Managing these first weeks carefully is an important part of cultural integration, but the process is not over just because we've hit day 100.

Over the course of the next year, employees will continue to integrate into the buyer's culture, becoming subject to the acquirer's policies and practices. These include performance management, succession planning, learning and development, compensation reviews, and so on.

If businesses aren't fully integrated, questions about talent mobility are likely to arise at this point, with leaders wanting to understand how to move employees between various parts of the business. These can be challenging conversations and often require assistance from labor and benefits experts.

This sample timeline is designed to give you a starting point for your overall cultural integration plan. It included several assumptions that might not line up to your specific deal. Be sure to validate any assumptions in your final plan with the integration team to ensure alignment.

Chapter 23: Measuring Cultural Integration

Measuring cultural integration is one of the biggest challenges in mergers and acquisitions. The HR M&A Roundtable asked Teri Zeinz, a graduate student in The Chicago School of Professional Psychology's industrial/organizational psychology program to formally research this topic. We've also hosted several meetings to discuss best practices. Our research and discussions have shown that very few organizations are happy with how they measure integration success.

As much as we would love to offer the perfect cultural integration scorecard, we can't. However, we can provide some suggestions for measuring cultural integration and suggest some ways to drive continuous improvement in deal outcomes.

Deal Success Metrics

The overall success of an M&A deal is traditionally measured through the achievement of financial goals. These goals and their results are seldom communicated to the HR team, making it difficult for HR to discuss how culture contributed to the deal's financial outcomes. Furthermore, the sobering reality that 70 to 90 percent of all deals fail to meet their financial outcomes makes this a challenging metric to adapt for cultural integration purposes.

Another common measure of overall integration success relates to project management outcomes, essentially measuring if programs and activities are deployed on time. For HR, these milestones include getting employees on pay and benefits on time, mandatory training completions, getting goals into the HRIS, and so on. While it's important to know if deal milestones are met or missed, it's difficult to tie meeting project timelines directly to the success of cultural integration.

Another common success metric, and one that's frequently used to measure the HR function's performance, is acquired employee retention. While it's quite a bit easier to get a raw retention percentage, it can be difficult to determine whether a specific number is good or bad without benchmark data that's difficult to obtain. It can also be challenging to understand why employees are leaving and whether they are related to culture clash. It's also difficult to use this raw number to drive improvements in HR processes when there are many factors contributing to employee exits that are out of HR's control.

Furthermore, employee retention can be a false positive. If the target's A players all leave, but the C players all stay, it's hard to call that victory. A better measure might be retention incentive effectiveness, in which the team measures whether employees who received a retention bonus decided to stay.

An emerging trend for measuring cultural integration success is via the pulse surveys covered in Chapter 15. By comparing the survey results over time, the integration team can see if acquired employees are starting to acculturate. However, employees are going through a lot of changes during M&A, and the survey should be seen as directional rather than definitive. Despite this limitation, pulse survey results are our best way to understand how employees are reacting to the culture change.

Driving Continuous Improvement

As we've seen, it can be difficult to measure the effectiveness of a cultural integration plan. Fortunately, it's much easier for an HR practitioner to evaluate their overall performance on a deal and evaluate opportunities for improvement using an after-action review, sometimes called a post-mortem.

To conduct the after-action review, the HR practitioner should evaluate the overall people goals of the acquisition. These goals often align with the metrics shared above, including achieving financial success (did we hit HR synergy targets?), hitting deal milestones (did people get their offer letters on time?), and retention outcomes (did we keep the people we wanted to keep?).

Once the goals are established, the HR practitioner can look at the steps taken to meet each of the goals. This requires introspection and conversation with other key stakeholders. This question can sometimes lead to finger pointing, which isn't productive. It's important to focus on what was done and why, not who is responsible if something went sideways.

Chapter 23: Measuring Cultural Integration

Once you've established what steps were done and why, review the outcomes. If the goal was met, ask what key actions drove successful attainment of the goal. If the goal was missed, ask what could have been added or done differently that would have increased the chances of success.

Finally, use what you've learned to improve the process for next time. This includes updating any HR M&A playbooks that might have been used in the deal process.

The after-action review process is a powerful tool for doing better deal work and isn't limited to cultural integration.

Conclusion

As we've discussed throughout this book, *company culture is how people get things done at work.* It's an expansive concept that's difficult to measure and manage because it touches every facet of an organization. It's also critically important to get right as we have countless examples showing that culture makes or breaks deals.

We know how to identify the key drivers of culture clash and understand how to evaluate deal-specific factors to find out where cultural problems are likely to emerge.

We understand what goes on in employee's heads and hearts when they learn about an acquisition. We know the importance of dealing with employee's identity crisis and uncertainty-related stress before asking them to tackle culture change. And we have a basic roadmap for re-recruiting employees, helping them gain certainty and adopt a new identity.

What Comes Next?

This book was never intended to be a comprehensive look at culture in mergers and acquisitions, but it contains everything you need to start the important work of overcoming culture clash. As you work through cultural integration on your deals, you will have questions and challenges that can't possibly be contemplated in this short work. You will need to balance company culture with regulatory requirements and emergent business needs. You will contend with leaders who don't value the work of cultural integration and employees who will resist change no matter how perfectly you implement your plan. And you will

Klint C. Kendrick

experience the rush that comes from getting it right – knowing you've made a difference for your business and the employees.

As you go through these challenges, you don't have to do it alone. The HR M&A Roundtable is a group of practitioners teaching practitioners how people, leadership, and culture drive M&A deal value. We offer a variety of free and paid options to improve your skills as an HR M&A practitioner, including in-person meetings in several major cities, virtual roundtables, high-quality training, coaching, and an annual conference. To learn more about the support we can provide you, visit our website at www.MandARoundtable.com. We invite you to learn from and contribute to our community.

My Best Advice

This book ends with the best advice I can give.

A few years ago, I gave a presentation on HR due diligence at HR West, one of the largest HR conferences in the United States. During the Q&A portion of my presentation, a seasoned HR practitioner stood up and said, "I'm overwhelmed. There is so much to do. What is the one thing I should focus on?"

I took a moment to think and replied, "The most important thing isn't on any of my slides. The most important thing to focus on is trusting your instincts. You are an experienced HR practitioner and your leadership would not have given you this job if they didn't think you were up for it. Trust yourself!"

I'm giving you the same advice: ***Trust Yourself!***

You can do this! and the HR M&A Roundtable is available to help if you need us.

Acknowledgements

During Egypt's New Kingdom, a young scribe took reed to papyrus and penned a prayer to Thoth[1], the god of wisdom and writing. Among the author's desires was the ability to clearly offer valuable advice to people who will benefit from it. While that ancient writer and I are separated by 3,000 years and 6,000 miles, our hopes and intentions are very much the same – sharing useful information that benefits our communities.

Ensuring that the effort required to write this book led to a useful practitioner's guide required a great deal of time and effort from a phenomenal group of people committed to making M&A work for everybody. If we met our goal and you find this book useful as you work to overcome culture clash, it will be due to the efforts of the small team who made this project possible.

Brendan McElroy is the HR M&A Roundtable's community manager whose work as student researcher uncovered the five main drivers of culture clash.

Another talented student researcher, Teri Zeinz, performed the primary research into measuring cultural integration, and her insights are included in Chapter 23.

Steve Steckler, who co-chaired the HR M&A Roundtable's past conferences and helped grow the Roundtable community, generously offered his insights into making cultural insights actionable.

Finally, this book would not be possible without the HR M&A Roundtable community itself, with many members sharing their stories and experiences, successes and failures, all in service of elevating the practice of HR M&A.

I continue to be grateful for my writing team, including book coach, Suzanne Doyle-Ingram, who provided much needed encouragement and expertise. My two best friends and readers, Nick Literski and Bryon Sobczak, reviewed early drafts to make sure the concepts were accessible and useful. Darcy Jayne, the amazing copy editor, had the difficult task of unifying the book's tone with a consistent look and feel. Scott Allen ensured the illustrations supported key concepts.

Finally, my most heartfelt gratitude goes to my husband, Scott Lindauer, who supported me through writing a second book, knowing that it meant our weekends and evenings would be punctuated by the sounds of me muttering at my laptop. My gratitude also goes to my children, Koyle, Kayden, Kaleb, and McKenna, and their mom, Sarah-Anne, for continually inspiring me to do my part in making the world a better place for their sake.

About the Author

Klint Kendrick has worked in human resources for over two decades, with extensive experience in mergers and acquisitions, international HR, people analytics, total rewards, workforce planning, diversity and inclusion, and employee engagement, recruitment, and retention. Dr. Kendrick has worked in multiple environments, ranging from HR leadership roles at Fortune 500 companies like SC Johnson, Oracle, and Boeing to being an HR department of one for scrappy start-ups.

Klint holds a Ph.D. in Organizational Leadership and a master's degree in Industrial/Organizational Psychology from The Chicago School of Professional Psychology, an MBA from California State, and an undergraduate degree in business from Eastern Oregon University. He holds designations as a Six Sigma Green Belt, Senior Professional in Human Resources (SPHR), and Senior Certified Professional by the Society for Human Resource Management (SHRM-SCP).

Organizations like The Conference Board, Bloomberg BNA, Thomson Reuters, McKinsey, Mercer, Willis Towers Watson, Transaction Advisors, MergerWare, Midaxo, M&A Science, and DealRoom have invited Klint to share his insights on the human side of M&A. Post-event surveys show that audiences find Klint friendly, engaging, and knowledgeable. They appreciate how his highly interactive style drives both conceptual learning and practical application.

Dr. Kendrick is a firm believer in professional development and has worked to ensure HR professionals can benefit from formal training, mentoring, and peer-learning. You can learn more about Klint at www.MandARoundtable.com.

About the HR M&A Roundtable

The HR M&A Roundtable is a peer-learning forum for Human Resource professionals working on mergers and acquisitions. We provide a safe and confidential environment where members share their lessons learned and best practices. The Roundtable isn't associated with any outside company but is driven by its practitioner members.

Dr. Klint Kendrick started the HR M&A Roundtable after several HR practitioners noted that our unique organizational cultures and the very nature of our work make it difficult to pilot new ways of supporting our organizations and acquired employees. This makes HR M&A an ideal discipline for roundtable learning.

Members are encouraged to share openly but are required to honor their non-disclosure agreements and other professional obligations. No confidential or sensitive information may be shared with the roundtable. To encourage open sharing, roundtable meetings operate under the Chatham House Rule, where participants may make use of the information shared by their fellow members, but they may not share the identity or affiliation of any speakers or members.

The HR M&A Roundtable offers a variety of free and paid programming, including face-to-face roundtables in Austin, Boston, Chicago, Dallas, Denver, India, London and New York. Virtual offerings include regular webinars, structured roundtable discussions, and networking happy hours. The roundtable also hosts an annual conference, where participants gather for two days to network and learn from one another.

For more information about joining the HR M&A Roundtable, visit www.MandARoundtable.com.

References

Introduction

[1] Quote Investigator (2017). *Culture eats strategy for breakfast.* QuoteInvestigator.com.

[2] Schein, E. H. (1992). *Organizational culture and leadership (2nd ed.), p. 12.* San Francisco: Josey-Bass.

[3] Cartwright, S. & Cooper, C.L. (1992). *Mergers & acquisitions: The human factor.* Oxford: Butterworth-Heinemann Ltd.

[4] Institute for Mergers, Acquisitions, and Alliances (no date). *Table 2: The size of the control premium and average value of a transaction by country.*

[5] Fernyhough, W. & Springer, R. (2020). *North American M&A report.* Pitchbook.

[6] Murphy, A., Tucker, H., Coyne, M. & Touryalai, H. (2020). *Global 2000: The world's largest public companies.* Forbes.

[7] Murphy, A. (2020). *America's largest private companies.* Forbes.

[8] NAICS Association (Feb. 2021). *NAICS links & resources: Counts by total employees.* NAICS.com.

[9] Sen, A. (Feb. 2021). *5 top realities why acquisition of entrepreneurial companies fail.* Fifth Chrome Consulting.

[10] Maxwell, J.C. (2008). *Leadership gold: Lessons I've learned from a lifetime of leading.* New York: HarperCollins.

Part1: M&A Basics

[1] Krouskos, S. (2019, October 14). *Why global M&A is expected to remain healthy into 2020.* EY.com.

[2] Engert, O., Kaetzler, B., Kordestani, K., & MacLean, A. (2019, March 26). *Organizational culture in mergers: Addressing the unseen forces.* McKinsey.

Chapter 1: The Deal Lifecycle

[1] Statt, N. (2021, January 13). *Qualcomm just bought a two-year-old startup founded by former Apple engineers for $1.4 billion.* The Verge.

[2] JustFood (2021, February 22). *Australia's Costa Group eyes citrus M&A.*

[3] Nolter, C. (2017, June 11). *Google, Apple and Facebook have always been obsessed with acqui-hires – here's why.* The Street.

[4] Lunden, I. (2020, October 15). *Stripe acquires Nigeria's Paystack for $200M+ to expand into the African continent.* TechCrunch.

[5] Clarion Energy Content Directors. (2021, January 5). *NRG completes $3.6B acquisition of Direct Energy.* Power Engineering.

[6] Harding, D. & Rovit, S. (2004, November 15). *Writing a credible investment thesis.* Harvard Business School.

[7] Schuler, R. S., Jackson, S. E., & Luo, Y. (2004). *Managing human resources in cross-border alliances.* New York: Routledge.

Chapter 2: Strategic Basis for M&A

[1] Burnett, G. M. (2020, January 10). *Analysis: U.S. M&A Mega Year in Review.* Bloomberg Law Analysis.

[2] Ibid.

[3] *Revenue synergies, cost synergies and consolidation.* (2015, December 18). Vehicle Service Pros.

[4] *T-Mobile overtakes AT&T as America's #2 wireless provider* (2020, April 6). T-Mobile.com.

[5] Hexatronic Group AB (2021, August 2). *Hexatronic strengthens Australian market presence through acquisition of two leading telecom businesses.* GlobalNewswire.

[6] Coren, M.J. (2019, July 12). *The staggering cost of self-driving cars is behind Ford and Volkswagen's new partnership.* Quartz.

[7] Boyle, A. (2017, February 10). *Ford partners with Google and Uber veterans at Argo AI for self-driving cars.* GeekWire.

[8] *U.S. Bank acquires Talech, gains digital capabilities as it transforms its business for the future.* (2019, September 9). Businesswire.

[9] Aguado, J. & Pinedo, E. (2020, October 6). *Update 1-Bank of Spain chief calls for more banking mergers to cut excess capacity.* Reuters.

[10] Romm, T., Zakrzewski, C. & Lerman, R. (2020, October 6). *House investigation faults Amazon, Apple, Facebook and Google for engaging in anti-competitive monopoly tactics.* The Washington Post.

[11] Meckl, R. & Röhrle, F. (2016). *Do M&A deals create or destroy value? A meta-analysis.* European Journal of Business and Economics.

References

[12] Martin, R. L. (June 2016). *M&A: The one thing you need to get right.* Harvard Business Review.

[13] Harding. D. & Rouse, T. (April 2007). *Human due diligence.* Harvard Business Review.

[14] Tortoriello, R., Oyeniyi, T., Pope, D., Fruin, P., & Falk, R. (August 2016). *Mergers & Acquisitions: The good, the bad, and the ugly (and how to tell them apart).* S&P Global Market Intelligence.

[15] Lewis, A. & McKone, D. (2016, May 10). *So many M&A deals fail because companies overlook this simple strategy.* Harvard Business Review.

[16] Chartier, J., Ferrer, C., Liu, A., & Silva, R. (2017, July 19). *Merge to grow: Realizing the full commercial potential of your merger.* McKinsey & Company.

[17] Chartier, J., Liu, A., Raberger, N., & Silva, R. (2018). *Seven rules to crack the code on revenue synergies in M&A.* McKinsey & Company.

[18] Jensen, M. C., & Murphy, K. J. (1990). *Performance pay and top-management incentives.* Journal of Political Economy, 98(2), 225-264.

[19] Hayward, M. L. A., & Hambrick, D. C. (1997). *Explaining the premiums paid for large acquisitions: Evidence of CEO hubris.* Administrative Science Quarterly, 42*(1), 103–127.*

[20] Cartwright, S. & Cooper, C.L. (1992). *Mergers & acquisitions: The human factor.* Oxford: Butterworth-Heinemann Ltd.

[21] Milano, C. (2015, September 1). *Bad influence: How well connected CEOs impact M&A results.* Risk Management.

[22] Berkshire Hathaway Inc. (2014). *2014 Shareholder Letter.*

[23] Viguerie, P., Smit, S., & Baghai, M. (2008). *The granularity of growth: How to identify the sources of growth and drive enduring company performance.* Hoboken, NJ: Wiley.

[24] Ryan, M. (2015). *Is 2015 a game changing year for divestitures?* Touchpoint by Firmex.

[25] IBM Investor Relations. (2019, April 4). *IBM to divest select software products to Centerbridge Partners.* IBM.

[26] Feiner, L. (2019, July 9). *IBM closes its $34 billion acquisition of Red Hat.* CNBC.

[27] Vengattil. M. (2020, October 8). *IBM to break up 109-year old (sic) company to focus on cloud growth.* Reuters.

[28] Vincent, J. (2020, October 9). *IBM will spin off legacy business to focus on cloud and AI services.* The Verge.

[29] Scully, J. (2019, February 15). *Coca-Cola revenues hit by bottler refranchising efforts during 2018.* FoodBev Media.

[30] *GE to lose majority control of Baker Hughes with up to $3 billion share sale.* (2019, September 11). CNBC.
[31] Carey, N. & Krauskopf, L. (2015, April 9). *GE to sell bulk of finance unit, return up to $90 billion to investors.* Reuters.
[32] Chesto, J. (2020, April 1). *Danaher completes acquisition of GE Healthcare's Life Sciences division.* Boston Globe.
[33] *T-Mobile closes deal with DISH to divest Sprint prepaid business.* (2020, July 1). T-Mobile.

Chapter 3: Culture Makes or Breaks Deals

[1] Dealogic. (2015, December 28). *Dealogic data shows 2015 M&A volume surpasses $5 trillion.* PR Newswire.
[2] Aliaj, O., Fontanella-Khan, J., & Massoudi, A. (2020, December 31). *M&A rebounds sharply to hit $3.6tn in 2020.* Financial Times.
[3] Nishant, N. (2021, December 30). *Global M&A volumes hit record high in 2021, breach $5 trillion for first time.* Reuters.
[4] Isom, P. J. (2021). *2021 was a blowout year for M&A – 2022 could be even bigger.* KPMG.
[5] *Concerned about the outlook for private equity in 2021? Don't be.* (2020, December 3). Investable Universe.
[6] Sim, B. (2021, March 2). *The record boom in blank-cheque firms could make 2021 the year of the spac (sic).* Financial News.
[7] *M&A in 2021: An accelerating rebound?* (2021, February 8). Morgan Stanley.
[8] *Global M&A industry trends.* (no date). PwC.
[9] Watson, R. (2021, February 19). *Survey forecasts busy year for M&A deals.* Grand Rapids Business Journal.
[10] Harding. D. & Rouse, T. (April 2007). *Human due diligence.* Harvard Business Review.
[11] Engert, O., Kaetzler, B., Kordestani, K., & MacLean, A. (2019, March 26). *Organizational culture in mergers: Addressing the unseen forces.* McKinsey.
[12] Ibid.
[13] Tibergian, M. (2018, June 27). *Does culture really matter in M&A?* ThinkAdvisor.
[14] Hollingsworth, J. (2016, October 28). *Culture clash: why western companies are better at mergers than their Chinese and Japanese counterparts.* South China Morning Post.

References

[15] Iger, R. (2019, September 18). *"We could say anything to each other": Bob Iger remembers Steve Jobs, the Pixar drama, and the Apple merger that wasn't.* Vanity Fair.

[16] Barnes, B. & Cieply, M. (2009, August 31). *Disney swoops into action, buying Marvel for $4 billion.* New York Times.

[17] Kovach, St. (2012, October 30). *Disney buys Lucasfilm for $4 billion.* Business Insider.

[18] Schwartz, M. S. (2019, March 20). *Disney officially owns 21st Century Fox.* NPR.

[19] Berkowitz, J. (2019, December 16). *Disney's dominance of the 2019 box office means its takeover of movies is complete.* Fast Company.

[20] Laporte, N. (2020, December 26). *The definitive ranking of streaming services as we head into 2021.* Fast Company.

[21] Whitten, S. (2021, February 11). *Disney says it now has 94.9 million Disney+ subscribers.* CNBC.

[22] Taylor, A. C. (2013 September). *Enterprise leader on how integrating an acquisition transformed his business.* Harvard Business Review.

[23] Hyken, S. (2015, December 5). *Drucker said 'culture eats strategy for breakfast and Enterprise Rent-A-Car proves it.* Forbes.

[24] Ibid.

[25] Taylor, A. C. (2013 September). *Enterprise leader on how integrating an acquisition transformed his business.* Harvard Business Review.

[26] Ibid.

[27] Andrews, E. L. & Holson, L. M. (2001, August 12). *Daimler-Benz to buy Chrysler in $36 billion deal.* New York Times.

[28] Finkelstein, A. (1995, April 12). *Chrysler takeover bid leaves workers nervous, glad Iacocca's involved.* AP News.

[29] McGarry, D. (2000, November 18). *DaimlerChrysler's culture clash.* MarketWatch.

[30] Maynard, M. (2007, August 12). *DAM-lerChrysler? If you say so, chief.* The New York Times.

[31] Ressler, D. (2020, March 5). *Remembering Jack Welch.* Intralinks.

[32] Lundberg. K. (1990, January 1). *General Electric and The National Broadcasting Company: A clash of cultures.* Harvard Kennedy School case study.

[33] Vise, D. A. (1985, December 12). *GE to buy RCA for $6.2 billion.* The Washington Post.

[34] Boyer, P. J. (1987, June 12). *GE tells NBC chiefs to change or go home.* The New York Times.

[35] Schweiger, D. M. (2002). *M&A integration: A framework for executives and managers.* New York: McGraw Hill.

Chapter 5: Deal-Specific Considerations

[1] Larsson, R. (2005). Synergy realization in mergers and acquisitions: A co-competence and motivational approach. In G. K. Stahl & M. E. Mendenhall (Ed). *Mergers and acquisitions: Managing culture and human resources* (pp. 183-201). Stanford, CA: Stanford Business Books.

Part 4: Planning for Cultural Integration

[1] Blumenthal, E. (2020, April 1). *T-Mobile closes Sprint merger after two-year battle.* CNet.

[2] Harding, D. & Rovit, S. (2004, November 15). *Writing a credible investment thesis.* Harvard Business School.

[3] Martin, R. L. (June 2016). *M&A: The one thing you need to get right.* Harvard Business Review.

[4] Patel, K. (2019). *Agile M&A: Proven techniques to close deals faster and maximize value. A practitioner's guide.* USA: Day1 Inc.

Chapter 10: Common Integration Scenarios

[1] Erlichman, J. (2019, October 23). *Three years after Microsoft acquisition, LinkedIn keeps quietly climbing.* BNN Bloomberg.

[2] TCS Education System. (no date). *Expertise.*

[3] Rivard, R. (2013, September 30). *The new 'system': Private nonprofit.* Inside Higher Ed.

[4] Gosselin, K. R. (2016, October 7). *First Niagara banks to become KeyBank this weekend.* Hartford Courant.

[5] Glynn, M. (2020, November 20). *How KeyBank's deal for First Niagara stacks up – five years later.* The Buffalo News.

[6] Deffenbaugh, R. (2017, May 19). *KeyBank Hudson Valley leader: First Niagara deal 'a case study' for bank mergers.* Westchester & Fairfield County Business Journals.

[7] Magaw, T. (no date). *2017 Archer Awards. HR team category: Public company (winner). KeyBank.* Crain's Cleveland Business.

[8] Kastrenakes, J. (2016, May 18). *Charter officially owns Time Warner Cable, creating the US's second largest cable provider.* The Verge.

[9] Charter Communications. (2015, May 26). *Charter to merge with Time Warner Cable and acquire Bright House Networks: Combinations benefit shareholders, consumers and cable industry.*

References

[10] Charter Communications, Inc. (2017, July 27). *Q2 2017 Results – Earnings Call Transcript.* Seeking Alpha.

[11] Farrell, M. (2016, May 30). *Charter's new road map.* Next TV.

Chapter 12: Acquired Employee Psychology

[1] Maslow, A. (1943). A theory of human motivation. *Psychological Review, 50*(4), 370-396.

[2] United States Department of Labor, Bureau of Labor Statistics. (2011, June 22). *American time use survey – 2010 results.*

[3] Seo, M., & Hill, N. S. (2005, December 1). *Understanding the human side of merger and acquisition: an integrative framework.* The Journal of Applied Behavioral Science.

[4] Kim, D. (2019, December 2). *Mismatch: Why workers don't stay after an acquisition.* Kowledge@Wharton podcast.

[5] Krug, J. and Shill, W. (2008), *The big exit: executive churn in the wake of M&As.* Journal of Business Strategy, Vol. 29 No. 4, pp. 15-21.

Chapter 13: Employee Communications

[1] Illes, K. & Mathews, M. (2015, February). *Leadership, trust and communication: Building trust in companies through effective leadership communication.* Westminster Business School

Part 6: Employee Listening

[1] Marinescu, I., Klein, N., Chamberlain, A., & Smart, M. (2018, March). *Incentives can reduce bias in online reviews.* Working paper 24372, National Bureau of Economic Research.

[2] *2021 Work Trend Index: Annual Report.* (2021, March 22). *Microsoft.*

Chapter 15: Pulse Surveys

[1] DiLeonardo, A., Lauricella, T., Schaninger, B. (2021, May 10). *Survey fatigue? Blame the leader, not the question.* McKinsey.

Chapter 18: Stay Interviews

[1] Moss, D. (2011, June 29). *Predict turnover with 'stay' interviews.* Society for Human Resource Management.

[2] *Please don't go! Companies conduct stay interviews to keep key people.* Challenger, Gray & Christmas, Inc. survey.

Part 7: The First 100 Days

[1] Illes, K. & Mathews, M. (2015, February). *Leadership, trust and communication: Building trust in companies through effective leadership communication.* Westminster Business School.

[2] *Ninety-eight percent of U.S. managers want better management training, Grovo study says.* (2016, September 28). PRWeb.

3 Dunbar, R. I. M. (1992). *Neocortex size as a constraint on group size in primates.* Journal of Human Evolution.

Chapter 19: Managing Employee Transitions

[1] Marks, M. L., Mirvis, P., & Ashkenas, R. (2017, March-April). *Surviving M&A.* Harvard Business Review.

Acknowledgements

[1] Mark, J.J. (2016, November 17). *Prayer to Thoth for skill in writing.* World History Enyclopedia.